TORNADOES

*Grief, Loss, Trauma,
and PTSD*

*Tornadoes, Lessons, Teaching —
The TLT Model for Healing*

Yong Hui V. McDonald

TORNADOES, LESSONS, TEACHINGS: HOW TO RISE
ABOVE GRIEF, LOSS, TRAUMA, PTSD USING THE TLT
MODEL

Books, audio books, DVDs written and produced by Yong Hui
V. McDonald are also available. To purchase, contact
www.griefpathway.com or order by phone: 1-800-booklog,
1-800-266-5564.

GriefPathway Ventures LLC, P.O. Box 220, Brighton, CO 80601.
Adora Productions is an imprint of the GriefPathway Ventures
LLC. Website: www.griefpathway.com.
Email: griefpwv@gmail.com

Published by Adora Productions
Printed in the United States of America
ISBN: 978-1-935791-09-6
First Printing: November 2011
Cover Design by Lynette McClain
McClain Productions, www.mcclainproductions
Cover Art & Design Copyright ©2011 Adora Productions
Some authors names have been changed by their request.

1. Grief 2. Trauma 3. PTSD 4. Spiritual Healing 5. Inspirational

CONTENTS

DEDICATION
ACKNOWLEDGMENTS

Chapter 1: How Did This Book Come About?...................7

Chapter 2: The Causes of Tornadoes...............................8

Chapter 3: Tornadoes, Lessons, and Teaching Model......10
1. Tornado...10
2. Lessons...12
3. Teachings..14

Chapter 4: What is Your Tornado?...............................16

Chapter 5: My Tornadoes and Healing
1. Tornado of Accident..19
2. Tornado of Panic Attacks.......................................19
3. Tornado of Disappointment....................................21
4. Tornado of Grief...25
    "FINDING PEACE" by Laura Padilla.......................28
5. Tornado of Grief and Making Peace........................29

Chapter 6: Tornadoes of Trauma and Fear....................37
"THE TORNADO AND LESSSONS" by Julia Roberts.....39

Chapter 7: Tornado of Suicide.....................................52
1. "IS SUICIDE WORTH IT" by Lakiesha Vigil.............53
2. "I TOLD HER GOOD-BYE" by Virginia Diaz.............56
3. "GIVE ME STRENTH" by Amanda Ramirez.............57

Chapter 8: Tornadoes of Grief and Loss
1. "I AM LETTING YOU GO" by Russett Loucks............59
2. "A BETTER PLACE" by Raelyn Santoya....................59
3. "REST IN PEACE" by Brandy Rodriguez...................61
4. "HEAVENLY BODIES" by Sandra Norris...................61

Chapter 9: Tornado of Accidental Death
1. "THE LESSONS I LEARNED" by Robert Garcia..........64
2. "THE ANSWER" by Mireya Vizcarra............................65

Chapter 10: Tornadoes of Trauma & Betrayal...............69
"I PRAY FOR MERCY" by Kristin Madril......................70

Chapter 11: Tornado of Homicide.............................75
1. "THE LESSONS" by Donna Tabor.............................75
2. "FORGIVENESS" by Nedra Walker............................77
3. "LIFE CHANGED FOREVER" by Mary Smith............80

Chapter 12: Tornadoes of Abuse and Addiction
1. "SOUL SEARCHING" by Dee Anderson..................86
2. "SEARCHING FOR LOVE" by Richard Schmittal......92
3. "GOD'S OWN MEDICINE" by Francesca Cayou........99

Chapter 13: Tornadoes of War................................105
1. "RESTLESS YEARS" by Bob Birx............................105
2. "WALK OF FAITH" by Bob Carr............................106

Chapter 14: How to Process Grief and Loss................110

Chapter 15: How to Process Trauma.........................116

Chapter 16: Spiritual Healing: Nightmares, Hurtful
        Voices and confusion............................... 122

Chapter 17: Victory Prayer..................................127

Chapter 18: An Invitation....................................130
1. An invitation to accept Christ............................130
2. An invitation for the Transformation Project Prison
   Ministry (TPPM) & "One Million Dream
   Project"...131
3. How to purchase *Maximum Saints* books................132

About the Author..135

DEDICATION

I dedicate this book to our Heavenly Father, our Lord Jesus, the Holy Spirit, and all people who are grieving the loss of loved ones, and who have been traumatized by their life experiences and are in need of healing.

ACKNOWLEDGMENTS

My mother prays for me and my ministry day and night. I believe because of her prayers, God has blessed me and my ministry beyond my imagination. I thank God for her. She has been my cheerleader. I am also deeply indebted to my wonderful husband, Keith, who died in a car accident in July 2008, and is with the Lord. Keith brought healing in my heart and helped in the preparation of my ministry more than anyone else I've ever met. I also thank my beautiful children Fletcher and Nicole. May God bless them beyond their imagination in all areas of life.

My gratitude to all the following generous people who donated their time and gifts to make this book possible:

(1) All the ACDF inmates who contributed their stories.
(2) Drawings: Burnie and Richard Cordova.
(3) ACDF editors: Juanita Adams, Billy bob Bramscher, Don Burough, Cody Bushman, Kathleen Cooper, Heather Curtis, James Escalante, Robert Garcia, Amanda Gonzales, Richard Irwin, Joshua Langston, Irva Lenzini, Amanda Powers, Betty Read, Raelyn Santoya, Robie Sothman, Juanita Tamayo and Cannon Tubb.

Thank you also goes to Glenda Yeisley for helping edit this book. Thank you all for your hard work, support and encouragement.

Finally, I give glory to Jesus. Without Him, this book could not have been written.

Chapter 1

How Did This Book Come About?

On June 25, 2011, God asked me to write a book to help others who are grieving, traumatized and suffer from Post Traumatic Stress Disorder (PTSD), using the TLT (Tornadoes, Lessons, Teachings) model.

The lessons that have helped myself and others who are lost in a "tornado" come from my own personal crisis plus from my counseling as a chaplain at Adams County Detention Facility (ACDF) and at the hospital where I help many who are dealing with "tornadoes" in their lives.

I saw a pattern after I counseled many people in crisis from grief, loss and trauma. Some were blown away by the tornado and were stuck in pain. Some, however, learned to process their pain, resolve the crisis, and then were able to move on. Those who moved on had similar patterns. They learned the lessons from their tornadoes of life. They became stronger and started helping others with what they had learned.

The TLT model was developed in my counseling to encourage people to focus beyond the tornadoes in their life. By focusing on the lessons learned through the tornadoes they experienced healing that helped them move on. Many who are stuck in pain and trauma, who have participated in this model, experienced an amazing recovery and are processing their pain allowing them to move on. In fact, I use the TLT model personally whenever I face any challenges. It's very simple and it works.

This book does not replace professional or pastoral counseling that you might be involved in and it doesn't replace your medication. However, learning the TLT model and reading other people's tornado stories, and how they process them, will give you time to reflect on your own tornadoes. Healing is a process; the TLT model can facilitate that process.

Chapter 2

The Causes of Tornadoes

No one is exempt from tornadoes in life. Life is not free. We pay a price for living, and that price is facing tornadoes from time to time—some are small but some are very big (hurricane sized.) Some are easy to handle but some are overwhelming. How we handle and manage our tornadoes will determine whether we will grow and come out strong, or whether we will stumble, fall, and get stuck in pain and grief. If we don't know how to process tornadoes in life, they will immobilize us and we may continuously be stuck in the storms of life. This is a bad place to be. Let's look closely at what causes tornadoes in our lives.

There are seven areas that can cause storms. Sometimes we experience several at once.

The Cause of "Tornadoes"

(1) <u>Ourselves</u>: Some troubles in life are caused by ourselves— failure in good judgments, immaturity, selfishness, bad temper, violence, low moral values and addictive lifestyles. Our poor choices can throw us into hardships and can cause debt, incarceration, or loss of everything which affects not only ourselves but our families and loved ones.

(2) <u>Our Family</u>: Our family members' low moral values, incarceration, addiction, selfishness, bad temper, violence, critical and judgmental attitudes, words and actions. Though we may not have done anything wrong, these actions of family members create turmoil and pain in our lives.

(3) <u>Others</u>: Painful events can be caused by other people's selfishness, critical attitudes, words and actions which affect us. If we come in contact with them at the wrong time in the

wrong place, it can be devastating to us.

(4) <u>Environmental Hardships</u>: You can be affected by the environment in which you live, who you are, where you were born and what country you live in. Many other factors over which that you have no control are: cultural and moral values, religious backgrounds, economic conditions, education, job skills, inherited genetic weaknesses, war, plagues, gender, and the color of your skin, etc.

(5) <u>Natural Disasters</u>: Floods, earthquakes, famine, volcanic eruption, tornadoes, hurricanes, storms, etc. These are all beyond our control.

(6) <u>Spiritual Tornado</u>: Torment and pain caused by spiritual attacks from the devil or evil spirits. It brings spiritual confusion, oppression, pain, turmoil and bondage. When we are freed from demons, we will be healed from torment and pain. When Jesus cast out the demon from the man who lived in tombs and was hurting himself, he was healed from destructive behaviors. He came into his right mind and took care of himself instead of hurting himself further.

(7) <u>Divine Tornado</u>: Sometimes God will let people go through hardships to teach them lessons. When Jonah was disobedient and running away from the Lord, God sent the storm in the sea to get his attention. When Jonah was thrown in the sea, God prepared a fish to catch him. Jonah, in his suffering, repented inside the fish. Some people perceive incarceration as a wake up call and God's intervention because if they were outside, they may have been hurt badly or even ended up dead.

Chapter 3

Tornadoes Lessons Teachings Model

1. TORNADO

A tornado in life is caused by a crisis which we all face. Life is hard, and whether we want it or not, we all face our share of crisis either small or large in our lives. Sometimes one crises can create many crises, like a ripple effect. Any life crisis can throw us into this unpleasant state. If you are in a tornado stage, you may experience turmoil, pain, fear, confusion, conflict, anger, devastation, disappointment or discouragement.

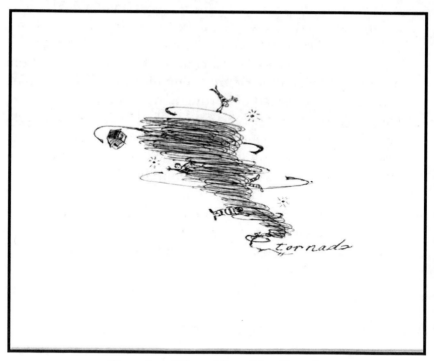

Drawing "Tornadoes" by Burnie

When you enter a tornado zone, you may be asking yourself the following:
(1) Why is this happening to me?
(2) What did I do to deserve this?
(3) This is happening to me because I am bad.
(4) Why didn't I listen to the warning of others?
(5) I am angry at God for letting this happen to me, etc.

How do people react to a tornado? Some may be upset, angry, and may blame someone or be confused. Many don't know how to land safely after they are thrown into the air. Some may fall onto a rock and be hurt. Sometimes they may have a safe landing if they learn to process their hurts and pain with new perception.

EXERCISE:
Reflect and answer the following:
(1) Who caused this tornado?
(2) What was the cause of it?
(3) What was my first reaction?
(4) What was my emotional response? Resentment, anger, disappointment, discouragement, betrayal, etc.
(5) How did I cope with the pain and emotional turmoil?
(6) Did I cause any other tornadoes after I was hit by this tornado?
(7) Is there anything God is trying to tell me through the tornado I am experiencing?

2. LESSONS

Staying in a tornado is very painful. We need to process and learn why it has happened, what lessons we can learn from it, so we can come out a stronger person. Therefore, whenever I face any tornadoes in my life, I process them as soon as possible. I try to understand why it happened, who is responsible for it, and what the lesson is I need to learn, so that I can move on to teach others what I have learned. You are invited to do the same. Understanding the causes of them will help you to learn what to avoid in the future. When people decide to learn the lessons, they begin the healing process.

Drawing "Lessons" by Burnie

EXERCISE:

Pick one incident where you experienced a tornado. If you can, share it with others whom you can trust or write it down and reflect to see what you can learn.

(1) What's the lesson I can learn from this?
(2) How can I experience healing from this?
(3) What do I need to do to find peace through this?
(4) Is there anything I need to adjust or change — attitudes, perception or behaviors — in order to process and heal?
(5) Do I need to forgive anyone and let go of my resentment or anger?
(6) What helped me the most in my difficult time?
(7) Have I had any regrets in dealing with this challenge?
(8) Is there anything I can do to prevent the same thing from happening to me in the future?
(9) What is God trying to teach me through this?

Each tornado has lessons to teach us. If we can learn the lessons, we can graduate from each tornado class and move on. We will learn what to do when we are hit by the same tornado the next time and how to process it.

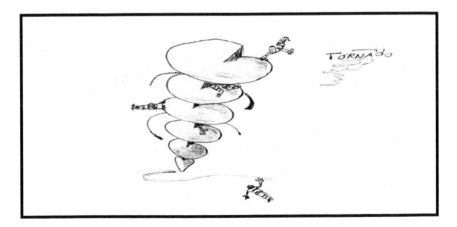

Drawing "Tornadoes" by Burnie

3. TEACHINGS

Those who have learned lessons from hardships have lessons to teach others. A little child does not have lessons to teach an adult about hard life lessons because they have not yet gone through the storms in life. Only those who have gone through life-changing experiences caused by tornadoes have learned lessons they can share with others.

Start focusing on what kind of lessons you may have for others who are going through the same problems. Our pain and suffering have lessons to teach us and others as well.

Drawing "Teachings" by Burnie

EXERCISE:

Reflect and try to answer the following:

(1) What can I teach myself and others with my tornado experience?

(2) Is there anything I can do to help others avoid the same pit falls?

(3) What do I need to do to help others? Is it sharing, writing my story or being involved with some kind of ministry?

This process gives directions to people as to what they can do with what they have learned to actively help others.

Chapter 4

What is Your Tornado?

There are many tornadoes but the following list gives you some ideas where you are. Reflect and find out how many tornadoes you are dealing with now.

(1)   Grief—You are grieving from the loss of your loved one from death, divorce or separation.

(2)   Health problems—You are diagnosed with an illness.

(3)   Trauma—You are traumatized by events such as physical, emotional, mental, or sexual abuse.

(4)   Incarceration—Loss of freedom, loss of self-respect, separation from family, losing children to social services, divorce caused by incarceration, losing a car or house or other things that you value.

(5)   Family incarceration—Your family is incarcerated.

(6)   Mistreatment by others—You are hurting because of hurtful and destructive words or actions by others.

(7)   Lack of resources—You feel you are running out of energy, resources and ideas as to how to handle problems in life.

(8)   Lack of mentors—You feel you are desperately in need of help, but don't know whom to turn to for advice or solution.

(9)   Emotional pain— Suffering from anxiety, panic attacks, anger, torment, resentment, etc.

(10) Unforgiveness—You are upset, angry or hateful, and cannot forgive those who have hurt you.

(11) Financial difficulties — You are having financial problems and you see no way out.

(12) Losing a job — You have lost jobs and cannot find employment.

(13) Depression — Lack of energy, helpless and hopeless

feelings, suicidal thoughts.

(14) Lack of love — Your family or significant people in your life don't seem to value you or treat you with love and respect.

(15) Addiction — You are suffering from alcohol, drugs, or sex addiction.

(16) Your family's addiction problem — Your family is suffering from addiction and you feel helpless about it.

(17) Lack of direction and purpose in life — You don't know the purpose of your life.

(18) Lack of fulfillment in a job — Lack of education keeps you from getting a job that you would like to have.

(19) Cultural values — People around you don't value you because of the way you are shaped, your gender or skin color.

(20) Your own value system — You are having a difficult time valuing yourself.

All these things are tornadoes in life. The need is to learn to cope and value our life, learn lessons, and find peace in all situations.

I encourage you to start processing each area with the TLT model. Some areas will take time to process because you have to make changes and adjustments in your way of thinking, in habits, jobs or even education to find a job that you like. Whatever it is, change is something you have to make in order to process and learn the lessons from each storm in your life.

EXERCISE:
When you face problems in life, if you try to process all of them at once, it's overwhelming. Follow the process of the TLT model one by one and write down what you have learned and when you need to make changes — perception, lifestyle, your thinking process, etc.

If you feel stuck and immobilized, I encourage you to find a professional counselor, pastor or a chaplain who could help you. The sooner you process the problem, the sooner you will experience healing from it and you will be able to function normally.

I encourage you to find people who have gone through a similar situation and have moved on. Ask them how they processed their trauma from tornadoes in their lives. People who are in a tornado cannot help you. But those who have learned from challenging problems in life and are able to move on can be your encouragement and your teacher. Find them if you can and learn from them.

In addition, there are many "tornado" stories in the Bible, and you can learn how others have dealt with them and how they overcame them. Read the different stories in the Bible to learn from them.

Chapter 5

My Tornadoes and Healing

I will share my tornadoes and how God helped me in my crisis and taught me lessons, so I can teach others with my life experiences.

1. Tornado of Accident

In 2000, I was attending Iliff School of Theology and that year I went through the worst time of my life with many events that traumatized me.

In January, I had a car accident on an icy road. The road was covered with snow. A truck drove by and I couldn't see anything. I lost control of the car. The car bounced and started moving, going somewhere, but I didn't know where. I was frantically crying out to God for help. At the bottom of the hill, I saw two fence posts and the car went between them and stopped by a pile of dirt. God prepared me for this accident through dreams, and I was able to walk away from the accident with calmness. The car was totaled but I was not hurt. It was a miracle that I survived. I gained more confidence in God through that experience. Due to that accident I began having panic attacks on icy roads. It was unexpected and I never thought I would have this kind of problem.

2. Tornado of Panic Attack

Before I had this accident, I had already had three accidents on icy roads. Up to that time, I never understood what a "flash back" meant. When I had a panic attack, my heart started racing, it became difficult to breath, my body started to stiffen. It was as if I was reliving the moment of terror when I had the accident.

My worst fear was that I might get into another accident or die because of my panic attacks. I prayed and prayed. I was fine as long as the roads were not icy, but I ran into many storms and icy roads. Sometimes I drove on dangerous roads where I couldn't see the road, only reflectors. I couldn't turn around because I couldn't see anything and it would be more dangerous. I was commuting 430 miles to school from Buffalo, Wyoming, to Denver, Colorado, for three years. Sometimes, I would cry while I was driving because of fear that I might get in an accident on an icy road. I ran into so many storms with bad roads in Wyoming.

How did I handle panic attacks? I started praying to God for His protection. I knew I should be ready to meet Him at any time, in case I died on the road. I prayed, "Because of your grace, I came this far. Help me, Lord, so I can drive safely." I prayed and prayed until my heart started beating normally.

LESSON:
The lesson I learned is that there are consequences when a person goes through any trauma such as an accident. Even though God prepared my heart, my body still remembered what had happened and my brain sent me warning signals which I didn't need. The trigger is icy roads and bad weather. I had to develop a coping plan and I did the following.

(1) Avoid driving on icy roads as much as possible.
(2) Find strength through prayer.
(3) Proclaim victory and healing in every aspect of my life.
(4) In those days I wrote a good-bye letter to each member in my family and carried it in a backpack in case someone would find me dead on the road. I thought it would be best to prepare for the worst.

TEACHING:
What can I teach others who are experiencing panic attacks? I developed a victory prayer in my personal, family and ministry life because of panic attacks. I gained strength from prayer. If I feel anxious about anything, I pray this victory prayer. I haven't

had any panic attacks since then. The victory prayer I wrote to calm my heart helped many others and was published in others books, but I will include it in this book as well to give you some idea how you could write your own prayer and find peace and strength.

3. Tornado of Disappointment

In December, 2000, God encouraged me to write about my spiritual experiences and how He started a revival in my heart.

At first I had no desire to write. I was suffering from many tornadoes in my life at that time: financial problems caused by my poor decision to buy more than ten houses was one of those. The housing market went downhill and our family suffered a lot from it. It was my mistake to go out and buy all the houses when God called me to the ministry. God tried to help me by telling me to sell my rentals when the housing market was good, but I didn't listen to Him. Although I had no control over the housing market, I felt so bad about what was happening. It was a humbling experience for me as well.

Also, my husband was having problems with our teenage children and our family was going through many tornadoes. All of us suffered. As I look back, we were all guilty of not being considerate of one another. On top of that, I was dealing with the fear of having panic attacks on icy roads. And the lack of family support for my decision to go into the ministry was very difficult for me.

My heart was broken and I badly needed the Lord's help. One day I couldn't even get out of bed. I felt like I was dying. I was deeply depressed. I tasted a little death that day. I had never felt that much disappointment and discouragement in my life.

I used to get up early and go to the church to pray, but I hadn't done that for about two weeks. That did not mean I did not pray. I went to church and prayed during the day. But I knew that was not good enough. God was urging me to focus on the Lord and pray more in the mornings.

Then I had a devastating dream. The sky was clear. I did not see anything. But a powerful force like a tornado was advancing toward our town. It was destroying many homes in our neighborhood. I was terrified when I saw houses and people thrown out into the air. I was hoping it would stop so we would not have to pack up and run, but the unseen force kept moving toward our home. My family was in panic. We frantically tried to decide what we should take with us. After I woke up I asked the Lord for understanding of the dream.

He replied, "My daughter, what you have felt in your dream will be felt by many who do not believe in me. The disaster is coming to many who don't know me and they do not realize it. Stay awake and pray so you do not fall into temptation. You cannot accomplish anything for my kingdom without praying."

It seemed everything was going wrong except my prison ministry. I was organizing prison ministries at school and took many students to minister in eight jails and prisons while attending school. That was the best thing while I was in school. I was so blessed with my ministry, but my home life was a disaster.

Finally, I started writing and it became a turning point in my journey of faith. It took me three weeks to write the book, *Journey of Mystical Spiritual Experiences* then later republished as *I Was The Mountain*. By the time I finished the book, God revived me with hope more than I had imagined.

My situation didn't improve and still I had the same tornadoes, but I was encouraged by God's leading in my life. Moreover, I felt blessed by how God has led me in the past and I was able to let go of resentment and forgive.

I concluded that I was supposed to serve the Lord no matter what happened or what others said. I would be disobedient to the Lord if I listened to others. After I focused on God's grace instead of tornadoes, I felt as though I had a shield around me to protect me from disappointments in life. That shield is my faith in Jesus. I found hope in Jesus Christ in the midst of turmoil and pain.

As I look back, this experience strengthened me to stay on the course of my call to serve the Lord. The next year, my husband's congregation would also try to discourage me so that I would quit my ministry. By then, God strengthened me so no one was able to stop me from my decision to stay in ministry. Since then I have experienced many more hurts, pains, grief, losses and disappointments in life. But every time, God pulled me out of it. He brought healing and revived me with hope.

LESSONS:
I have learned many lessons from this experience. First, the Lord taught me what He can do with my little faith. I had faith that everything would turn out alright because God was leading my ministry. The Lord has all the resources to help me and can heal wounds, heartaches, pains, disappointments and discouragements. He brought healing in my heart so I was able to rely on the Lord for strength to go on.

Second, He taught me how to be content. I need to focus on what I have and not on what I don't have. Focusing on what we don't have only brings discontentment. Therefore, the Lord taught me to let go of my expectations and dependency on others. I learned that if I expect more, I will be experiencing that much more hurt and pain. People can give me only 5% but I expected 85% from them. No wonder I was on the road to disappointment. I also learned that others expect 85% from me when I can give only 5%, so, I learned to accept human limitations and let go of my expectations.

Third, I learned that when tornadoes come I need to focus on Jesus, so He can help me in times of trouble. He is a great example of how to calm the sea. He said, "Be still." I need to do the same by proclaiming victory and healing for my family. We can experience healing in our hearts and find peace in God even when the situation has not changed. I was changed and grew spiritually through these difficulties. We can be shielded from disappointment and discouragement when we rely on Jesus.

Fourth, reflections and writing helped me to learn about God's greatness and brought healing. I never realized that writing could heal my broken heart but it did because it helped me to focus on what God can do and not on what I was going through. Just looking at the tornado, the problems overwhelmed me. But looking at the Lord while I was writing gave me confidence that He would help me get through it, and He did.

Fifth, problems in life are a purifying fire. It showed what I was relying on: people and material things more than the Lord. I finally realized that my problems can be solved when I put my priorities in the right place. Loving and serving God has to be my first priority. When I finally decided to seek God and His kingdom, I had peace. Outside objections didn't matter. How others treated me didn't matter. That was an important lesson I had to learn in order for me to continue my journey with Jesus.

TEACHING:
First, God is going to help you no matter what situation you are in. We need to have faith in God all the time.

Second, find contentment through God. Read the Bible and pray to find comforting words from the Lord. People or things cannot provide contentment. So, don't expect anything from others. If they give you 5%, thank them instead of being angry. If they don't give you anything, still thank them for being there.

Third, Jesus gives you peace. People or things do not. God has eternal plans for us so don't be discouraged in any circumstances. Problems in life are temporary and they, too, will pass.

Fourth, without tornadoes in life, our faith cannot grow. Thank God for teaching you what's important in life when problems come.

Fifth, even when we try to do something good, others may misunderstand us and we may not receive any support but following the Lord is what we need to do in any circumstance. When God asks you to do something, don't expect that others will understand you. Obey the Lord even though others may not understand it.

Finally, reflect and write how God has helped you in the past and what He wants you to learn from this. There is a lesson for each tornado that comes. When we learn the lesson, we can help others who are in similar tornados so they may learn how to move on.

4. Tornado of Grief

Losing my husband in a car accident in 2008 was another traumatic experience I went through. Keith was my husband for 30 years and I was unprepared for his sudden death.

I was immobilized with grief and suffering from triggers of pain. God told me that as long as I was holding on to my husband, I would not be free from pain and triggers caused by grief. I didn't know that holding on to my husband would cause me to be stuck in a tornado. God was right.

I was helping other grieving people and told them to let go of their loved ones, but I was holding on to my own husband. If it was up to me, I would still be immobilized with pain because I thought holding on to my husband was honoring him.

I finally let my husband go by giving him to the Lord and asking the Lord to take away all desires and hopes related to him. God answered my prayers and I was healed from pain. Within three months after my husband's death, I was healed from grief; that was a miracle. Since then, I don't even miss my husband any more and I don't suffer from triggers of pain caused by my husband's death. When I shared that, other people had a hard time believing it, but it happened.

LESSONS:
God can lead us in our grief and losses and bring healing. But I had to do my part and process all the emotional issues related to my husband's death: resentment, forgiveness, blame, attachment, anger, etc.

I learned that the sooner I take care of all the painful emotions, the sooner I could experience healing. I did that by writing a journal of what made me sad and break down, then what brought healing. That was necessary for my healing, but I couldn't graduate from grief and pain caused by my husband's death until I followed the Lord's instruction to let my husband go.

When I focused on what I didn't have, which was my husband, I would grieve everyday and that's not what God wanted me to do. He told me my grieving was becoming a hindrance in my walk with Him.

God wants to bring healing to our broken hearts. Losing someone that you love doesn't have to immobilize you for the rest of your life. God can heal our grieving hearts and triggers of pain. He wants us to be well and be happy instead of grieving for the rest of our lives.

TEACHING:
While I was grieving I couldn't help others because I was self-absorbed and lived in self-pity. Again, God didn't want me to live in self-pity, but instead focus on Jesus to find meaning and purpose in my life. In order for me to focus on loving the Lord and serving the Lord, I had to be healed. When I was grieving, I had to stop all my writing projects and I was not able to function normally. My mental capability was limited to focusing on what I had lost not what God wanted me to do.

After God healed me, I was able to go back to writing books and started helping others. I finally realized why God didn't want me to stay in the tornado of grieving and continuously break down, because that was a life of misery. God didn't want me to live in misery and pain. I found peace and joy after God healed my broken heart.

I have learned so much about grief and healing that I started GriefPathway Ventures, LLC, to reach out to others who are immobilized with pain from grief and loss. I have been helping many who are grieving with many lessons I have learned from the Lord, especially how to process grief and healing step by step.

Interestingly, I always wanted to write a book on grieving because I have met so many grieving people in my ministry at the jail and at the hospital. But I wasn't able to do it until I lost my husband. I learned that God can use our tears and painful stories to bring healing to others.

Losing a loved one is a devastating tornado we have to go through, but it happens to all of us if we live long enough, and sometimes it happens without warning. But God can bring healing when we learn to focus on Him and ask for help and let our loved ones go.

To help others who are grieving, God directed me to write a book, *Dancing in the Sky, A Story of Hope for Grieving Hearts*, about how God brought healing from the loss of my husband. This was something I had not planned to write but it's because of God's leading hands, I was able to write it. The day my book was finished, God told me to make a DVD to help grieving people. I produced *Dancing in the Sky, Mismatched Shoes* with my husband's last congregation.

Actually, I didn't quite understand how my book would help others but God used it to touch many. I will share how God uses our stories of tears and bring healing in others.

One day I got a phone call from Laura Padilla and she shared how much my *Dancing in the Sky* book helped her. God told her to donate $1,000 to Transformation Project Prison Ministry, so she did. I visited her to see how she was and I was blessed to meet her. I thought she may be rich to donate $1,000 but when I visited her, I was reminded of a widow who gave everything she had. Laura lost her job at the time but God was asking her to donate. I was deeply moved by her story. She had gone through a tornado of grief and loss and she found healing. Here is her story.

"FINDING PEACE" by Laura Padilla

When my significant other, Jesse, committed suicide two and a half years ago, I was lost and felt I had no other outlets but to dwell in my own guilt. We were together for 16 years. I didn't understand why we had two children. Now they had to go through life fatherless and I was alone so I turned to drinking as a way out and made poor choices. I didn't even recognize myself anymore. I always thought I was a strong individual who took care of my family, but I was so lost. I didn't know what to do. It took me to dark places. Sometimes I thought there was no way out. I believed I had done something really bad to have this happen to me.

I gave my life to the Lord years ago but for some reason I didn't feel God's love. Because I was so numb, I would not open myself up to it. Therefore, I started praying and praying because all I could think about was Jesse's salvation. One early morning in October 2009, the morning star was shining on my house and God gave me peace. At that point I started going back to church, praying more and reading my Bible, but there was something still missing. I didn't know what it was.

On Mother's Day 2010, my son gave me a book called, *Dancing in the Sky*. I read it and was amazed how inspiring this book was to me. It has helped me in ways I didn't know were possible. My grieving was hindering my relationship with God which was what I was missing. I needed to give Him all my attention and not to my iPod listening to sad songs reminiscing on the past.

When I first lost Jesse my sister used to give me advice. I was so mean to her and would tell her, "You don't know what I am going through unless you have experienced it. If you know someone who has gone through it and come out of it in one piece, and they have the joy and peace in their life, that is the person I want to talk to." To be honest I never thought there was a person in this world like that until God brought Yong Hui McDonald in my path. She is an amazing woman and an inspiration to all.

I am so grateful for the book *Dancing in the Sky*. I no longer have that pain in my heart. I am able to talk and share things about Jesse that I was never able to do before without breaking down because I had a big hole in my heart. There is joy now that I never thought I would have. I have been sharing this book with family and friends and anyone who crosses paths with me. God is amazing and He can heal your broken heart. You gotta give it all to Him. Thank you and God bless!

Laura's testimony greatly encouraged me. God can bring healing in times of grief and loss. I thank God that He was able to use my story.

5. Tornado of Grief and Making Peace

I learned that there are four areas in which I needed to find peace as part of my grieving process: Peace with God, myself, my husband, and with other people. I found peace with God, my husband and myself, but I had not had the chance to make peace with the people who were involved in the car accident with my husband. My husband made a mistake turning left and there was an on-coming car. There were three teenagers in the other car. They all were hurt and one was seriously injured. About nine months after my husband's death, I received a card and letters from them. This is what I have received.

"Sorry about your loss, I hope you can forgive, and sorry about my writing. I have a cast on it because of the accident. We all are sorry about the whole thing."

"I am 14 years old. I was one of the boys in the other car that collided with Mr. McDonald's truck. I will never forget when the two cars collided, that was probably the worst, most horrible thing I've ever experienced. I got the worst out of it from everyone in our car. I was hospitalized for two weeks. I would tell you what all happened to me and all I had to go through but it's too long to write on a piece of paper. I am terribly sorry about your loss, we all feel really bad. When we found out we all started crying. My friend found out before I did. I didn't find out till around two hours later, right before I was going into surgery. I wish there was something we could all do to help out. We feel really bad about the whole thing just because of the fact it's our first accident and someone passed away. I know this card isn't going to make you happy about your husband but I hope it helps you feel a little bit better. Hope you are doing better."

"I was the driver of the other car. I'm 17 turning 18 on the 25th of September. I'm really sorry about everything that has happened. I wanted to let you know if I could have done anything to prevent that from happening, I would have. I'm doing better now. I had a fractured collar bone that is recovering. I wanted to let you know if there is anything that we can help you with we all would be more than happy to do what we can. We were going to hand deliver our notes and cards but my mom said it might be too much for you to handle. I hope you are doing good. Sorry about your loss. When I found out that your husband passed away, I felt terrible and I cried because I thought it was my fault for his passing. Sincerely."

After I read these three young people's letters, I was touched by their thoughtfulness, but felt like I was reliving my grief again. I never thought that I would go though so many tears after I had experienced healing, but I did. There was more healing needed in my making peace with everyone. I cried for many days. I wasn't ready to respond to them but I felt bad the driver of the other car was suffering from guilt which was not his fault. I asked my friend Laura to write a letter on my behalf. She told me I needed to write it myself. I was praying for these young people's healing and God helped me to write on 5-11-09, ten months after my husband's death. Here is the letter I wrote to the driver of the other car.

Thank you so much for the card and the letter. The day I received the card and read your letter and your friends' letters, I was flooded with tears. I was crying more than the day my husband died. I was in such shock when I first found out my husband had died that I didn't feel anything. Now, I am more aware of what it means to lose someone, and that makes it hard.

There are many things in life that I wish hadn't happened. This accident is one of them. What made me sad is that one mistake can take a person's life and can cause so much pain in others.

You and your friends are very kind to write letters to me. You all are still in pain and traumatized, yet wanted to help me. Your mom was right. I am not ready to see anyone who would remind me of my husband's death. In fact, I didn't think I was ready to respond or write a letter to you at first. I felt like I was reliving my pain and grief. I asked my friend to write a letter on my behalf. I wanted to let you three know that I appreciate the card and letters. I was told that I need to write, and I agreed; so I asked God to help me. Here it is.

I felt really bad about what happened to you three, especially you. I cannot imagine how anyone went through what you have gone through. Even though it wasn't their fault. Anyone who got involved in an accident would feel bad if someone died. All I can say is that I am grateful that no one else died as a result of this accident, even though you all are still struggling with pain and recovery.

I can assure you that I have no harsh feelings toward anyone about my husband's death. In fact, I feel bad that you have to go through this painful guilt trip which you don't even deserve. My husband made a mistake which cost him his life. I ask for your forgiveness on behalf of my husband because if he hadn't made a mistake, you three wouldn't be in pain. I am sure my husband feels bad about what happened to you three. I know my husband's heart. He would have helped you in any way he could. There was no way he would have hurt you. However, he made a mistake and unintentionally hurt you and your friends, please forgive him. I pray that God will bring healing to you and your friends.

I struggled so much after my husband passed away, but I have many supportive friends, and God has helped me. I am able to go on with my life though I still have more grieving to go through. There will be two different memorial services for my husband in June when all the pastors from Montana and Colorado get together. In July, my family is going to take my husband's tombstone to a cemetery and we will spread his ashes. I know this summer is going to be very difficult for me, my family, and many people who knew my husband. I thank God that I am surviving through this. I have faith in God that He will help me get through it.

God helped me to write a book about my story of grief and healing called, *Dancing in the Sky*. It will be published and will be coming out within a month. This book will help others who are grieving. God also helped me write a brochure to help others who are grieving. If you three would like to receive the book, please let me know. I will be happy to send one to each of you. I am enclosing the brochure in case you would like to read it. It may help you recover from this horrible experience.

In the brochure, I talk about making peace with

everyone. I have already made peace with God, with myself, and with my husband. One area I haven't been able to make peace yet is with those who were involved in the car accident.

You and your friends asked me what you can do to help. Actually, the card and letters you and your friends sent me helped me a lot, even though I shed more tears. Knowing that there are some people who are hurt but go beyond their own pain to think about other's pain and try to do something to relieve it, gives me hope. Your letters brought healing to me.

I would like to know whose idea it was to send a card and letters to me. It took lots of courage and wisdom to do it, and it helped me. If any one of you would like to meet me in the future, I will be glad to meet with you. You may call me and leave a message. I will get back with you.

Even though I am sad that my husband cannot be with me anymore, I gave him to God in prayer, and God has helped me. You all can let go of him as well. Ask God to help you with this terrible memory, so God can help you experience emotional and mental healing.

What will also help me recover is to know that you three young people will not be discouraged by this horrible accident and that you will eventually recover and come out stronger with God's help. I will be continuously praying for your healing and recovery.

I wanted to write a separate letter to each of you, but this letter covers it all. Would you please give your two friends a copy of this letter along with the brochures (their copies are enclosed). I want them to know that I appreciate their letters and concerns, and they don't have to worry about me because I have many people who support me and I have faith in God. Thank you for your letters, and God bless you.

Yong Hui McDonald

I sent the letter, but the letter was returned, unopened. I thought I had done my part, so I let it go. However, in December of 2009, God spoke to me that I needed to get a hold of these three young people.

I had already processed my grief and moved on. These young people, however, were still hurting by the accident and that could affect them the rest of their lives. They needed healing as well. Also, I needed to make peace with those who were involved with my husband's death.

I contacted Victims Advocates and asked them to make arrangements so I could meet with the three young men who were involved with my husband's accident, if they wanted to meet me. I asked the Victims Advocate to give them my book and DVD *Dancing in the* Sky and the letter I had written to them.

The meeting occurred in April, 2010, 22 months after my husband passed away. It was a very emotional day for me, but God knew we all needed to process this traumatic experience and needed healing and closure. I was able to meet them with their mothers present.

My son, Fletcher, wasn't ready to meet them because he was still grieving, but he came along with me to support me. I was glad he came because he, too, had to process grief and I thought this meeting would help all of us with closure.

I thanked them for the letters they sent me and also asked them to forgive Keith because if he hadn't made those mistakes, they wouldn't have been hurt mentally, emotionally, and physically.

They told me they had already forgiven him and they felt so bad and wanted to attend my husband's funeral, but they didn't know how I would have felt, so they didn't come.

I was encouraged and touched by their kindness. I asked them whose idea it was to write letters to me. I learned that it was the one who was seriously injured from the accident. I thanked them for their courage and compassion.

Meeting these young men provided closure to my grieving and healing process. However, I was troubled by how much these young men were struggling because of the accident.

These young men gave me hope—hope of seeing goodness in others. The next time we met, we shared more about the accident and what we all went through and we had many wonderful conversations.

LESSONS:
I learned that it's easy to look into our own pain and loss and forget about the pain and suffering of others. But God wants us to go beyond our pain. When God leads us to do something, we may not be ready to do it. But if we obey Him, it's always for our own good and the good of others.

There was no way I would have thought about meeting these young people because they were a reminder of my loss. But God knew it was necessary for me to meet these young people who were traumatized by the accident. We all had to process hurts, pain and trauma caused by the accident.

Also, I learned more about God's goodness through the thoughtfulness of these young people. That proved to me that God really wants to bring healing to everyone even in the midst of a tragic accident.

I am thankful for God's leading in this difficult process of learning the lessons of tornadoes of life. There is always hope knowing that God is with us and He is going to lead us onto the right path.

TEACHING:
Paul said, *"Make every effort to live in peace with all men and to be holy; without holiness no one will see the Lord. See to it that no one misses the grace of God and that no bitter root grows up to cause trouble and defile many." (Hebrews 12:14-15)*

It's important to make peace with everyone and to help each other to experience God's grace. These young people helped me to experience God's grace. I thank God for them. We can help others to experience God's love and healing power when we reach out to others who are hurting. Listen to your heart so you can follow the Holy Spirit to help others who need your help; who need your encouraging words.

I learned that my suffering is so small compared to what these young men are going through. They are still processing grief and some live in physical and emotional pain. But their goodness spoke to me loudly, that there is hope for them. I pray for their healing and fast recovery. I thank God for putting them in my path. I ask you to pray for others who are hurting and reach out to them.

Lastly, I saw good things could come out of tragedies and this is one of those cases. I got to meet three amazing young people who went beyond their own pain and loss. I thank God for teaching me the lessons from these three young people. Ask God to see positive things in your suffering. God has plans for all of us and can use our painful experiences when we can share how God brought healing in our hearts and lives.

Chapter 6

Tornadoes of Trauma and Fear

The day God asked me to write a book to help those who are suffering from grief and PTSD as well as sharing the TLT counseling model, I couldn't believe it. So, I asked the Lord to give me a sign that He really wanted me to write on this subject. Writing this book was not on my list even though I counsel people who suffer from PTSD daily. Whenever God asked me to write a book, He had good reasons, so I figured that He would show me His reason. I was working at ACDF that day.

By the end of the day, I still didn't get any signs why I should write this book. Then as I went to visit a housing unit, a deputy asked me to visit Julia Roberts who had serious problems. "Can you visit her everyday and check on her?" Normally, when a deputy asks me to visit an inmate, they don't ask me to visit them everyday. I felt there must be something really serious happening with this woman. We have about 1,400 inmates, and depending on the case, I rarely visit anyone every day or not even every week.

I met Julia in the contact room and asked her how she was doing. She shared about how her life had been traumatized with one event after another. Prior to that meeting, Julia came to the chaplain's worship services and also to the prayer meetings whenever I led them in the housing unit. I didn't know her very well until that time.

I listened to her horrific stories and how she suffered. She was traumatized to the point that she couldn't handle even seeing males in the hallway. One of the female deputies told me that she had to clear the hallway if she saw any males while she was escorting Julia to her housing unit. She was traumatized to the extreme. The deputies could hardly believe how much this woman was tramatized. I thanked God that I had met Julia. She was the answer to my prayer that I should write this book to help others who are suffering like her. Here is her story.

The First Session:

Julia was a tall, soft spoken woman. She shared her story of the horrors of sexual assault by a stranger who slashed her throat and left her for dead. That was just the beginning of her long years of agony, pain, and suffering. On top of it, she was pregnant. She had tried to abort the baby, but she wasn't successful. When the baby was born, she couldn't bear to watch because the baby was the reminder of her rape and assault. She eventually gave her daughter up for adoption. Julia suffered from so much pain and trauma that she started taking some classes to help herself. The class has helped her somewhat but she still suffers from painful memories, and as a result, she has a difficult time seeing or getting close to any men.

After I heard about Julia's story, I drew TLT models and explained to Julia that her condition is more like living in many tornadoes and she needs to process each one and learn the associated lesson, and that she can then help others by making the lessons into a teaching model. I explained to her that when someone is thrown into the sky by a forceful tornado, there is a lesson for all of us. We can process lessons by starting to share or write stories: first tornado stories; second lessons; third the teaching we have for others.

I asked, "Julia, do you think you could write your life story based on a TLT model? Write your tornado story and the lessons you have learned and how you can teach others. This will help you to experience healing in some areas. You have gone through many tornadoes and you need to process all of them one by one in order for you to experience healing. This will be a good way to begin."

She said, "I haven't tried to write my story but I will try," she replied.

I explained, "*Mark 16:18* says, '*When they drink deadly poison, it will not hurt them at all*' and I don't interpret this

Scripture literally but symbolically. My understanding of poison in this context can be interpreted as those who have experienced trauma, tragic losses and hardships because of it. A tornado which is so damaging, like poison, entered into their souls and immobilized them. They can be very sick and some may even feel like dying, but with God's help they can be revived and be healed by focusing on the lessons that they have learned which can teach others. The lessons we can learn in life crises are found in the Scriptures. God's Word has all the answers for the healing of our souls. I prayed with her to gain God's wisdom to process healing from all her hurtful, terrifying experiences.

The Second Session:

When I met Julia the second time, she read what she wrote for me. She told me she followed the TLT format and it actually helped her while she was writing her story. Here is what she wrote.

"THE TORNADO AND LESSONS" by Julia Roberts

My tornado started as a child. I come from a family of ten. I have seven brothers and two sisters. Growing up for me was not easy. I was like the black sheep of the family. You may as well say that I wasn't born at all. I had no one to love me at all and no one to talk to out of all the brothers and sisters I had. I was all alone in this dark world. "My father," Lord only knows where he was.

My mother raised us by herself. The boys were her favorite. Lynn and I were the only girls. My mom gave her away when she was two and I was four. That hurt me so bad. I'm all alone, no one knows and no one cares. I went to school sometimes when my mom had the time to comb my hair and get me ready.

I was tired of hurting on the inside. At the age of 14, I ran away thinking it would be better for me to live by myself. I started out being raped, sleeping with everybody and anybody, just to have some where to stay. I met this guy and had my child at the age of 15. Trying to go to school and raise a baby was not easy at all.

My baby's dad used to beat me and make me have sex when I didn't want to. I felt dirty all the time, I couldn't get clean for anything, I hated it. I was being raped almost every night. Wow! Another baby. It's a boy. This time I'm around 17 years old. By the same guy but he swore it was not his and started beating me again. I got tired of that too. So, here I am on my own.

I had another girl but she was stillborn. I asked God, "Why?" *"Blessed are those who mourn, for they will be comforted."* (Matthew 5:4) *"They dress the wound of my people as though it were not serious. 'Peace, peace,' they say, when there is no peace."* (Jeremiah 6:14) I tried again to replace that hurt, but nothing could bring back that little girl I had lost. So, I started getting high. I got pregnant again with a boy. I really didn't want another baby because I couldn't take care of the two I had, so I gave him away to a family. They raised him to be a good young man.

Not knowing my son, really hurts me. *"My people are destroyed from lack of knowledge."* (Hosea 4:6a) I have seen my son two or three times. I was running from my pain, not knowing that God is really there. I was selling my body and doing drugs.

Things got rough, so I left and went to Texas and got raped in 1994. I have scars to remind me of everything I went through and I also have a baby girl. She is now 15. When I was carrying her I really didn't want her at all because she was a rape baby. I did everything I could to get rid of her but God said differently. *"Freely you have received freely give."* (Matthew 10:8b)

By placing God first in my life, I realize that everything I have is a gift from Him. You realize that your life is not dependent on material things. It's dependent on God. I went through the storm with my own child. I couldn't stand to look at or have her around me. So, I gave her to the Wacon Methons

Homes. She had a foster mother who took good care of her while I was locked up.

I got out of jail only to mess up again. I didn't want this child. I was raped. I felt shame and hurt having a baby. A baby from a rape is very hard to deal with because you think they are different, but they are not. I had to face my consequences no matter what. I had to be still. *"Be still, and know that I am God; I will be exalted among the nations, I will be exalted in the earth." (Psalm 46:10)*

God's guidance and direction can take you anywhere you want to go. Just pray for God's perfect will for your life so if you think you are standing firm, you can be careful that you don't fall. *(1 Corinthians 10:12)*

I thank God everyday for my life and her's, too. I thank God for putting this child where she needs to be. I have love and understanding in my life so I can see that she is really a blessing from above.

"Father God, I thank you for being my light and my salvation so whom shall I fear? I will fear no evil for you are with me. You lead me in a path of righteousness. You prepare a table before me in the presence of my enemies. For day and night your hands are heavy upon me; therefore let everyone who is godly pray to you while you may be found. Be still before the Lord and wait patiently for him, know that the Lord is good. Enter His gates with thanksgiving and His courts with praise. My heart is steadfast, oh God; I will sing and make music with all my soul. Amen."

While I was listening to her story, I was touched. I asked, "How many times did you have to write to finish this story?"

"I just wrote it once," Julia said.

"You are a gifted writer," I said, "You don't know how many times people have to write a story like this. I am very impressed with your writing. I can assure you that God will be able to use your stories of tears, pain and tornado to help many others who have gone through similar experiences. Your story will teach others how to process their horrific experiences and teach them to be strong and rely on God for healing. God is going to use you. You have a calling."

"Actually writing this helped me a lot," she said.

"I have the second writing assignment for you. Can you write how you found God and how He has helped you? This will help you focus on your spiritual journey and how God brought you healing so far."

"Sure, I will try to write it," she replied.

Julia was able to concentrate and articulate her thoughts to process her hurts and pain. I saw a gentle, kind woman who had gone through many storms because of abusive situations, yet she did not want to give up. Her story indicates that she needs to process many different issues to get out of the tornado stage.

The Third Session:

I typed her first story and gave it to her so she could edit it if she needed. When she saw her typed story, I saw the smile on her face. This time Julia gave me a story about her spiritual journey.

"WHY GOD?" by Julia Roberts

I found God while I was locked up. I needed a friend and someone that loved me. I needed someone that I could share my dark secrets with. I humbled myself and asked God to come into my life. I had to let go and let God have His way with me.

I always knew that there was a God but I couldn't understand why bad things were happening to me. So I asked a question, "Why God, why?" There was a time when I wouldn't admit that I was a sinner, but today I am entirely ready to have God remove everything that is not of Him out of my mind, soul and my spirit because I know He cares for me. Jeremiah 29:11 says, *"'For I know the plans I have for you,' declares the LORD, 'plans to prosper you and not to harm you, plans to give you hope and a future.'"*

My Lord says through this Scripture, "I want you to enjoy success. I do not plan to harm you. I will give you hope for the years to come. When I kept silent about my sin, my body became weak because I groaned all day long. Day and night your heavy hand punished me. I became weaker and weaker as I do in the heat of summer. Let everyone who is godly pray to you while they can still look to you. When trouble comes like a flood, they certainly won't reach those who are godly."

I said, "You are my hiding place. You will keep me from trouble. You will surround me with songs sung by those who praise you because you save your people."

The Lord tells me through the Scriptures: *"I will instruct you and teach you in the way you should go; I will counsel you and watch over you." (Psalm 32:8)*

And that's God. He is real! I suffered from painful emotions. I had contact with others and I didn't know if they were okay or had STDs or maybe AIDS. I felt like I was dirty all the time because of my contact with others. I thought nobody loved me and that's why bad things kept happening to me.

My question was if there is a God why are bad things happening to me? Is it because I'm not walking my walk with God? Am I being faithful to Him like I should?

"God, you said that you will never leave me or forsake me." He answered my questions through the Scriptures and continuously brought healing to my broken heart. I learned that I was saved by God's grace. The following Scripture helped me to have faith to focus on His grace and not my failure and sin.

"Through whom we have gained access by faith into this grace in which we now stand. And we rejoice in the hope of the glory of God. Not only so, but we also rejoice in our sufferings, because we know that suffering produces perseverance; perseverance, character; and character, hope." (Romans 5:2-4) "Let us then approach the throne of grace with confidence, so that we may receive mercy and find grace to help us in our time of need." (Hebrews 4:16) "May our Lord Jesus Christ himself and God our Father, who loved us and by his grace

gave us eternal encouragement and good hope, encourage your hearts and strengthen you in every good deed and word." (2 Thessalonians 2:16-17) "Humble yourselves before the Lord, and he will lift you up." (James 4:10) "Do to others as you would have them do to you." (Luke 6:31) "The thief comes only to steal and kill and destroy; I have come that they may have life, and have it to the full." (John 10:10)

Reflection

Julia started dealing with different emotions such as loneliness, shame, fear, anger and resentment. She recognize how she felt dirty and defiled. She felt bad, but she realized that God's grace saved her and the Scriptures helped her to have faith. She focused on His grace and not her failure and sin. Julia accepted her weaknesses, yet she understood God's grace shines in any circumstance.

I said, "You did a great job. I am so impressed with your story. I have the next writing assignment for you. This is a difficult one. Can you write a letter to your daughter and ask her to forgive you for not being able to take care of her and tell her how much you love her?"

Julia said, "Oh, that's going to be hard, but I will try to write it."

"Sometimes our healing comes when we understand others' pain. If you can focus on your daughter's pain and her need for a mother, it can bring healing to your heart and to your daughter's heart as well. After all, she is not here on earth because of you, but because God allowed her to be here. God gave her life, even though you bore her. Recognizing that she is God's precious creation can help you understand that you need to love her and not reject her. Her life is a gift from God. It doesn't matter how she was conceived."

"Chaplain, I am learning that she is here because of God. I tried to abort her but nothing worked. I learned that our life is a gift from God. I know God wants her here."

<u>The Fourth Session</u>:
The day I visited her, one of my Clinical Pastoral Education (CPE) supervisors was visiting me at the facility. Actually, prior to this meeting, I was told that Julia was not able to handle even seeing a man because seeing men were triggers of pain because of her rape and assault. So, when she came out I asked her if my CPE supervisor could be with us. Julia said it was alright. We met in the contact room and Julia gave me the letter she wrote to her daughter. Here is what she gave me.

My dear beloved child "Dominique,"
I love you more than words could say, Dominique. I want your heart to be made cheerful and strong. I know I have not been a mother or mom to you because of the way I had you. "Being raped is not a good thing."
"But God gave me a blessing and that was you." I love you and long for you. You are my joy and my crown. My love for you gets stronger everyday. I love you, little girl, with all my heart and soul. Please never forget that or think I don't. I love you. You are very special to me, but the Word of the Lord stands. We are going through the pain and suffering. Love is the purpose of God's command. Love comes from a good sense of what is right and wrong. It comes from faith that is honest and true. Jesus says, "I am with you always."
"I love you Dominique." There is a time for everything. There is a time to tear and there is a time to mend. And there is a time to love someone that's very dear. Love, Mom

After I read her letter, I was again amazed. Julia did a great job of writing a heart-warming love letter to her daughter. I told her I would type her letter and she could edit the next time.
Julia said, "After you type all my stories, I am going to mail them to my daughter so she can understand what I have gone through. I have been talking to her but we do not have a close relationship. She is 15 years old and is pregnant and she is

going to give her baby up for adoption. She is with my older daughter now but I don't know why she is not going to keep her child. I wasn't able to handle having her so I had to give her up for adoption. I believe sending her my stories will help her to understand me and I want to have a better relationship with her."

I said, "I am so glad that you are going to work on your relationship with her. She deserves her mother's love. I am glad that you are willing to make it happen."

"I am going to do it," she said.

"I am proud of you. Is your writing project helping you in your healing process?"

She replied, "I cannot believe how much it is helping me. It has brought so much healing. It changed my life. I couldn't even be around men but obviously I am doing much better. Here I am sitting with a man. I thank you chaplain for helping me."

I thanked her for sharing her life with me. I said, "I am very encouraged. I am also impressed by your knowledge of the Scripture."

When I saw her big smile, I knew God was leading her from destruction to hope and a new path not only for her healing but many others through her.

There are many areas that Julia still needs to take care of and her tornado stories need to be processed one by one. Julia started recognizing different tornadoes and wrote how she was processing forgiveness.

"FORGIVENESS" by Julia Roberts

You owe God your "life." You must let go of the pain of the past and move on. God has promised us a wonderful future! So, let go of the things we cannot change in our past. God said, "Look, I am making everything new!" And then He said to me, "Write this down for what I tell you is trustworthy and true." And He also said, "It is finished! I am the Alpha and the Omega, the beginning and the end."

There is hope for all of us, no matter how terrible our past or the problems we face today. God can make a way out of no way and it works every time. Indeed, the right time is now. Today is the day of salvation. There are times when we are so confused and overwhelmed by the pain we are facing. One thing that may make it hard to believe in God is that life often seems unfair to us. But God is on our side, even if we can't see it right now. But watch out! Be very careful. Never forget what you have seen, and what God is doing for you. May His miracles have a deep and permanent effect upon your life.

What a wonderful God we have! He is the Father of our Lord, Jesus, the source of everything merciful, and the one who so wonderfully comforts and strengthens us in our hardships and trials. And why does He do this? So that when others are troubled needing our sympathy and encouragement, we can pass on to them the same help and comfort that God has given us.

"Dear God, help me set aside all the hassles and noise of the world to focus and listen just to you for the next few minutes. Help me get to know you better and your purpose for my life. Father help me live within today, seeking your will and living this day as you would have me. It is my prayer to have others see me as your child, not just in my words but, more importantly, in my actions. Thank you for your love, your grace, your perfect forgiveness. Thank you for all those you have placed in my life, for my prayers were answered. Your will be done, not mine. In Jesus' name I pray. Amen."

Reflection

Julia recognized that she has a choice, she can learn from the lessons and move on to help others with the lessons she has learned or stay stuck watching the same tornadoes that she can see through the window of her heart.

If she doesn't go forward, she will be stuck in the same tornado and she will be playing the same scenes over and over, like watching a TV screen that doesn't stop and she will be traumatized by her past.

She was living in turmoil, pain, and trauma for more than 15 years. Julia is tired of being stuck in the tornado stage. Her daughter cannot get help from her mother as long as Julia lives in terror caused by the tornado of trauma and fear. Julia decided to move on by focusing on lessons and decided to help others through her stories. Here is another powerful story she wrote.

"I DON'T RUN THE SHOW" by Julia Roberts

I have learned that I can transform my mind. What we feed into our mind is the key. So, let the Word of Christ dwell in you richly. If we let His thoughts occupy our mind day after day we will grow in His likeness and begin to view life from His perspective. Now we must determine to follow through with new confidence and conviction and put that truth into daily practice. The response God wants is not just knowledge, but obedience. The Holy Spirit leads us in a closer walk with God. He brings out the reality of Jesus when we yield to a true spirit of praise and worship from our hearts; we then begin to change.

"Lord, God, almighty Father, I trust in you. You are my rock, my fortress, my deliverer, my God and my strength. I choose to trust in you with all my heart instead of leaning unto my own understanding. In all my ways I will acknowledge you and I know that you will direct my paths. Thank you for the truth Father. Your Word, oh God, gives me faith to trust you. Your word, oh, God, is forever settled in heaven. You watch over your word to perform it, your word never returns unto the void. It always accomplishes your purpose. I commit my way to you Lord, God, because I have put my trust in you. I will not fear what others can do to me. I will call upon you and I know you will hear me. You are my trust, almighty God. You are my hope. I look unto you continuously. I have chosen to trust you and I will remember your name Lord God. You are Jehovah Jireh, my provider. You are Jehovah shalom, my peace. My joy increases in direct proportion to my ability to trust you. Father, let me ever shout for joy because I trust in you. Thank you for the happiness that comes to me as I learn to walk in trust. Amen."

Reflection

I believe God did fast work on Julia because she was open to God and focused on what she can do with her painful experience instead of being stuck in pain. Her healing encouraged me so much I finally understood why God was asking me to write this book through her. With God, all things are possible and Julia's fast recovery is a gift from the Lord and also her decision to process her tornadoes which were destroying her life and her family, especially her daughter. She gave me the following note after she wrote her first story.

Letter from Julia Roberts

"I thank God for Chaplain McDonald for letting me share the things I've been through in my life. I feel more close to God than I ever have been in my life, today. Chaplain McDonald, I would like to thank you. At last I understand the hurt and pain and how God is using me to win souls. That's a blessing to me. Chaplain McDonald, never stop preaching God's Word because you are truly a blessing and I thank God for putting you in my path. And I know without faith, it is impossible to please God. I also learned that I cannot be one with Him and entangled in the world at the same time. God is good all the time.... Jesus said, *"I am the light of the world. Whoever follows me will never walk in darkness, but will have the light of life."* (John 8:12b) Thank you Chaplain McDonald for helping me." Julia Roberts

Reflection

Julia's letter encouraged me by using the TLT model, she has been reaching out to others. Again, this is a confirmation that what God has taught me is working. The TLT model can be effective when a person is open to process their tornado with God's help and through powerful healing Scriptures which Julia is doing.

"A THANKFUL HEART" by Julia Roberts

I never knew that life could be so unique when God has His hands around us. Jesus said, *"With man, this is impossible, but with God all things are possible. (Matthew 19:26)* I would like to thank God for my healing. How did He do it? God said, "You are safe with me. I am here to help you overcome the things that have happened to you." So, I started writing my story.

He told me to go down to the potter's house and I did. He took my old clay and broke it down and started to reshape me. I am a victim of rape, lost in sin, nowhere to run, nowhere to hide. But God was there helping me to become a new creation.

It was not an easy thing to do. I had to replay my life all over again. God said, "Just walk with me, follow my foot prints in the sand." He started rooting me from the inside out. He took away the feelings from being raped. He took away the bad feeling about men and myself. Then the Lord gave me a little girl. Then he took men and put them in front of me and said, "Come child, I am here."

From that day on, I have not been scared of being around men. I thank God for saving me. Let God reshape you. If you do this, you will experience God's peace which is far more wonderful than the human mind can understand.

Healing comes from God if you move yourself out of the way and let God reshape you. You will feel lighter. Now, your attitudes and thoughts must all be constantly changing for the better. So, this is a new beginning because God has healed my heart so I don't hurt so much inside.

And I know that God is my best friend. He healed me: Amazing grace, how sweet the sound that saved a wretch like me; I once was lost, but now am found; was blind but now I see.

"Humble yourselves before the Lord, and he will lift you

up." (James 4:10) For I can never forget these awful years I have been through, but God granted me the serenity to accept the things I cannot change and the courage to change the things I can. "Thank you Lord for walking in the sand with me. Create in me a pure heart, Oh God, and renew a steadfast spirit within me. God restores my soul. He guides me in the paths of righteousness for His name's sake. Blessed by the potter's hand. Amen." Jesus said, *"When Jesus spoke again to the people, he said, 'I am the light of the world. Whoever follows me will never walk in darkness, but will have the light of life.'" (John 8:12) "Then you will know the truth, and the truth will set you free." (John 8:32)*

Julia found purpose and meaning out of the suffering.

It's been less than two months since I met Julia. Her healing from the Lord and her willingness to work through her problems are visible. She is leading prayer and has preached in the worship services. She is shining in the darkness. I learned that she has been called to the ministry and she is a powerful leader and a prayer warrior. Praise God. She is encouraging others to walk in the path of faith so they can experience healing. Healing from trauma is possible through God's help when a person is willing to focus on what they can learn and what they can do with what they have learned. I thank God for bringing healing in her heart. Julia is gifted in many areas and many times when I lead prayer, she sings and prays. Her songs are anointed. God touches all of us. We feel the presence of the Lord when she sings and minister to us.

Julia has written many more stories and shares her faith and testimonies of faith, healing and hope. They are powerful because they comes from her experiences, the deep pain and healing she has experienced. I encouraged her to write her own book because her story will help many others. She can write one story at a time and then later she can publish it to help many more people with her stories.

Chapter 7

Tornado of Suicide

One of the worst types of death people deal with is suicide. I have met many who are shaken by the event and if they don't process it, it could be damaging to their mind and also their life. I know this because my father committed suicide and that tore my family apart. It was through God's grace that I was able to forgive my father and was able to move on. It's because of my family's suicide experience that I know people can be healed from the trauma with the help of God.

I also know what people go through when suicide happens. I have counseled many who have been affected by suicide at ACDF and also at the hospital, especially when I worked as an intern chaplain at Memorial Hospital in Colorado Springs, Colorado. Memorial Hospital is a trauma center and I dealt with many critical incidents. The lessons of how to help these people who are affected by suicide, through the TLT model, came after I counseled many critical incidents at ACDF.

Suicide is the highest form of death among prisoners and when it happens, it affects so many people. I was talking with three women who were affected by suicide and asked them to describe their tornado and the lessons they learned and how they can teach others. Three of them all came out differently.

One day I was leading a chaplain's worship service in D Module. In the middle of the worship service, I heard a scream and I didn't know what had happened until the deputy asked me to send the inmates back early from the worship because there was an emergency. After everyone walked out, the deputy told me that there was a suicide attempt in one pod. She asked me to talk to a few ladies who had found the woman's body.

I counseled two ladies and prayed for healing for them and also asked God to give the woman who tried to commit suicide a chance to recover.

The next day I was told that before this woman died, she was surrounded by loving family. They prayed together and she was able to communicate with them by squeezing their hands. They saw tears streaming down her cheeks. Her brain was slowly dying. The family eventually unplugged life support.

That afternoon, I had all the women from the housing unit in the contact room and gave the report and answered their questions to help them process this tragic event. I had many more sessions with different women who were affected by suicide and one of them was Lakiesha Vigil.

Lakiesha Vigil was the roommate of the woman, she was shaken by the event. I encouraged her to process her trauma by using the TLT model, so she could focus on what she could learn from this event and how she could help others with what she had experienced. She could write a story that would help people prevent suicide.

She told me she was stuck and she didn't know how to go forward with the story. So I asked her to write, "Is Suicide Worth It?"

She smiled and said, "Oh, that I can write. I definitely have something to say about that."

I was encouraged she was willing to write. I said, "It will help your healing process and also others who are suicidal to think twice about what they will do. If what you will write will help only one person to change their mind from suicidal thoughts, it will be worth it. But I believe it will help many people." This is what she wrote.

1. "IS SUICIDE WORTH IT?" — Lakiesha Vigil

I've been affected by suicide personally. I found my last roommate, hanging in our room. I've seen a lot of horrible things but never a person hanging two feet away from my pillow. I didn't know her too well considering I was with her only a week and she slept all day and night. All I knew was her name and she was a mother to three little girls, had a fiance, and also was a daughter, a granddaughter, and a sister.

The day I found her in our room, I was shocked, frightened and angry. Why was I angry at her? Well, first and foremost, suicide is a selfish act. She was only thinking about herself and not her children or family she was leaving behind, not worried how it would affect whoever would have found her, if not me. Her actions affected me tremendously.

I have to take medication to help with my thoughts and memory. My room door being closed, lights off, clothes hanging on the ladder, even blond haired girls were all triggers for me. I was afraid to walk in my room with the light off. I wasn't able to close my door or turn my light off during our time out. At first, I thought I could tough it out and stay in the same room, but I couldn't do it. I had to move out of that room. When I went to pick up my stuff, the clothes she used were still tied to the ladder. The image of her lifeless body replayed. I had to make sure that there were no clothes on the ladder after this. She had blond hair so every time I saw a blond head, I thought it was her. I hoped she was okay and alive. Wishful thinking!

One particular person I'd like to mention and thank for helping me get through this is Christine. I've known her a long time and lived with her before. That night I moved into her room. Oh, did I mention she is the only one who ran after me to help? Yes Christine had seen exactly what I did. We both frantically tried to untie her, hoping we could save her before the officers arrived. Christine and I helped each other get past the traumatic experience. The meds helped ease the intensity of the memories. Of course I know nothing can erase our memories for good, but meds do help. Christine respected my request, door wide open all the time, lights bright and nothing on the ladder. She never complained. Instead she told me she understood and when I was ready to make changes, they would be made.

"Thank you very much Christine. I greatly appreciate your support and help getting through this and lots more. God bless you." It's been three months since D's death. I've progressed on my healing process. I don't have those triggers anymore. I shut my door now. Not every blond head reminds me of D. Fortunately I haven't had nightmares or bad dreams about it. Whether it's the meds or simply a blessing, I don't know. But, hey, I have no complaints. I am just fine without them.

Meds weren't my only help. I couldn't have coped without my Heavenly Father. I believe "This too shall pass." Blunt, but super true. Only God can bring true healing. All you have to do is ask Him to help you. He already knows what you need. He just wants to hear it from your broken heart, out of your mouth. "Ask and you shall receive." Trust in Him. He will never let you down. The memories are here to stay, but through this experience I am hoping I can help one person to let go of a friend or loved one who committed suicide, or maybe even save his or her life from suicide by sharing my story.

Is suicide worth it? For many people suicide is the only way out, a permanent solution for a temporary problem; for these individuals nothing seems to go right. The stress is too much or the pain is unbearable. Rent money, car payments, losing a loved one, a bad break up. It becomes too much. "Do it, just kill yourself. Stop the hurt. You are not worth it. They are better off without you." The voices never rest. Very often people believe these voices and end it all.

These voices are the enemy. We are God's children. We must resist Satan's lies. He will work overtime to bring us to rock bottom. On our way down, he will make us believe we are horrible people. "God will never forgive your mistakes. God doesn't love you." These are his lies. The truth is God doesn't stop loving you. You are the apple of His eye. He will forgive your every sin and He does not remember them.

If suicide is the answer to every problem life gives, I'd imagine the world's population would be zero. Everybody would commit suicide. We all have problems. One thing people fail to realize is the affect suicide has on family and friends.

Even the people around you, people you don't know.

Losing a loved one is hard enough but losing to suicide is much harder. They wonder and ask, "Why? What if I could have saved him or her?" Suicide ends your pain and begins someone else's. So, if you are considering suicide, put all your pain, problems, and struggles aside and think for a minute about the pain and depression your family will endure. Ask yourself, "Is suicide worth it?" No problem in life is forever. Life may not be a piece of cake, but death is no sweeter. I was only a simple roommate but D's suicide traumatized me, now I am glad that God has helped me experience healing, so I could write this.

"Dear D, well, my friend this is my good-bye letter. I was so angry with you for all this, but I've forgiven you. I really wish we would have talked more but the few times we did we had some laughs. I know the Lord has forgiven you. I pray God gives healing to your children and lets them know mommy is always by their side and loves them very much. I also pray He helps J as well. And whoever else was affected. We will miss you, never forget you, forever love you. Rest in peace friend. Try not to eat all the pop-tarts. Good-bye, always your friend/ roommate."

What Lakiesha wrote was amazing. Her stories are published in many other books. She was recovering fast because she saw that she can learn the lessons and also help others with her story. I was very proud of her because I have never seen anyone who recovered from suicide that fast. She could have been stuck with pain and grief, but she was able to process them and was able to move on. Of course, her faith in God was helping her recover and her willingness to work out her emotions by writing her story to help others. What follows are more stories of pain, suffering and inspiration.

2. "I TOLD HER GOOD-BYE" by Virginia Diaz

I was at ACDF in 2009, in D Module. A friend hung

herself. We were good friends. I saw when they put her on the ground and worked on her. It made me very sad to see her like that. When I was released it went with me. I went to church and asked Father to help me. When I went to bed, I couldn't close my eyes because I saw her. It took some time to go away.

Now that I came back to jail on June 15, 2011, I came to see her again. She would call my name and say, "You are in the wrong room." She would pass my room and I saw her walk and touch me. I would ask God to put His hand all around me so I would sleep. I was moved to F Module. Now I can sleep good. I don't hear her or see her. I told her good-bye and said I would see her someday.

3. "GIVE ME STRENGTH" by Amanda Ramirez

A friend of mine committed suicide here at ACDF. She hung herself one day after I got bonded out. I found out from a mutual friend who was released a few days later. She called me and said, "Oh, my God, did you hear what happened to D?" I thought maybe she got out or into a fight. She told me that she killed herself. I couldn't believe it. I was in shock. I couldn't understand how she could just do it when she had little babies. We were not best of friends. We actually only got together to get high. When we were together, we always seemed to have fun.

Ever since I have found out about her death, I feel really responsible and guilty. I feel like she shouldn't have been there alone. I should have stayed in jail. Her kids will never see their mother. Since her death I have visions of D and I see her in her blue jail clothes, her face very blue, and her eyes red from crying. If I look at her face for too long, she starts looking very angry at me and her face changes as if the devil is in her and coming out of her.

I never have heard words from her. I have heard grunts. I have had her approach me and slam her hands on the table or area where I am at, but no speaking. I feel her always watching me and always see her across the way just standing there looking more and more angry. I feel as if she wants to tell me that I should be where she is at that I should be dead or that she is blaming me for her death. I don't know what else to do. I go to therapy once a week and speak to my therapist about her. I don't know why she doesn't just go away.

Everyone tells me it's not my fault. But it's not that easy to believe when you are in my position. I know in my heart I am not capable of committing suicide. I can't do that to my children. I now know that she died at the hospital and not in the jail. I have hope that she is safe in heaven with the Lord. I know it is just the devil tormenting me trying to pull me to him. I have struggles every day and I am trying to forgive. Hopefully one day I will find peace with myself and her death.

"Dear God, I so dearly need your help in my life. I am tormented from many things in my life. My mother's abandonment, the major life change of losing 350 pounds, leaving my husband, and losing my children. I feel as if I have ruined my life, my husband's life, my children's lives and the Lord from all my bad choices. I have now lost a friend from suicide. I am suffering everyday from all of these problems, I don't honestly know how much more I can take. I have heard that God only gives you what you can handle. Lord, I don't know how many more times I can ask you for strength to fight my addictions. Give me the strength to get my life back together. I want my life back, my family and my children. Lord, I want my happiness. I need peace with the death of my friend. Now I know she is with you Lord and I need the strength to fight off the temptation of the devil. Please Lord, I forgive everyone who has done wrong to me and I ask for forgiveness for all my wrong doings. Lord, I know I have done many wrong things. I have been led into temptations, but please make it easier to be able to go to the better things. I want a good life. I want happiness, please I beg of you."

Chapter 8

Tornadoes of Grief and Loss

1. "I AM LETTIN YOU GO" by Russett Loucks

I lost my dad when I was 16 years old. He was only 39 years old. It was the hardest thing for me in my whole life to face that he was gone. I did everything with him. Six months later, I lost my father-in-law in a car accident. When I lost my baby boy, I was ready to take my own life. Then I looked at my dog, whom I loved so much, and he saved my life. I was very mad at God because I felt He took my son then my father-in-law in a car accident six months later.

I blamed God so much. I have been through three deaths of very close people in my life. I don't blame God anymore. I learned that God didn't take them from me. We are here temporarily.

What helps me the most is God, reading Scriptures, and knowing that right now other people are going through even worse situations than I am. I have to thank God for being there and helping me. It took coming to jail to open my eyes and heart. It is kind of sad that people have to have devastating things happen to them to open their eyes and hearts to God. I am thankful because now I have the Lord Jesus in my heart. Also, I can't point a finger or blame anyone or anything for the troubles in my life.

"Dear Dad, I am letting you go. I am so mad at you for leaving me especially when I was so young. I know I need to let you go. I am also going to forgive you for all the times you spanked me and that you never really told me you loved me. I forgive you. I know you are with my baby Benjamin. It is comforting to know that my father-in-law, Dad, and my baby are all together in heaven. I miss you dad."

2. "A BETTER PLACE" by Raelyn Santoya

In May of 1998, on Mother's Day, I lost my father, my best friend, "my everything." He had been real sick with liver disease due to alcohol abuse. Through all this I lost myself into a life of destruction and to this day I am still not over the grieving process. I was so upset with my dad, the Lord, and most of all, myself. I blamed myself for many years because the last night I was with my dad when he was alive I prayed and prayed for the Lord to take my dad away so his pain and misery would be taken away. I wanted him to be free in that better place with God to start a new beginning. I am barely learning to forgive and stop blaming myself with the help of the Lord.

The Lord Jesus is the only way I am getting through this after 13 years. Before, I would use drugs daily to numb my heart and forget. But now it's time to let go and say good-bye so I can move on with my life for myself and my children because living in my selfish ways have has affected everyone that I love so much, especially my children.

"Dear Dad, it's been a long 13 years and I miss you so much and I never thought I would have to let you go completely, but as long as I keep holding on the longer my life is going to stay in this vicious cycle that brings nothing but pain and suffering to myself and everyone around that loves me, especially my children and my boys. That was a lot of the reason why I had been so upset with you dad, because you are not here to meet and be with your grandsons. G reminds me so much of you. We call him "Sonny" since that is what your nickname was. I want you to know I am sorry for all the hard trials I caused while you were here and for how our relationship was before you left me. Daddy, I am extremely sorry and I live in the pain everyday knowing that I never got a chance to tell you how much you mean to me and how much I love you. I do have to say I am not sorry nor do I regret praying for God to take you away because you are on to a better place, a place of no more pain. But Daddy now it's time to let you go so

I can grieve and forgive so I can move on with my life, move on with my family. Good-bye Daddy, I love you and miss you so much. Love, your daughter."

3. "REST IN PEACE" by Brandy Rodriguez

My little sister passed away 14 years ago in a car accident and we were very close. My sister and I ended up doing hard drugs, one year later my mom passed away. She was drinking, and as she walked across the street, a car hit her. I wasn't even over my sister's death yet so I hardly shed a tear. I mostly got angry and I still can't believe she is gone. Then a year later my grandmother passed due to drinking. I didn't even shed a tear. Then a month after, my other grandmother died of health issues and lots of close friends also have passed.

It is so hard for me to get close to anyone because I feel they will be taken away from me. I've even pushed away my children and turned to gangs, drugs, alcohol, and violence more than ever. I wish I could change, the Lord has helped me lately through all this. I've never felt the pain. I drank and used drugs to take the pain away since I was 17 years old. I've given my life to the Lord and I know I need more praying and I also need closure. Not having my kids is what hurts me the most because due to these deaths, I let my kids go and now I have a chance to have them back. The alcohol seems to have control of me.

"Mom, sister, grandmothers, please forgive me for being a failure, I forgive you mom and sister for leaving me. I feel so alone. I wish you guys were here so I could have someone that really loves me and I can talk to. Now I have my kids. Thanks to God. I love you. Rest in peace."

4. "HEAVENLY BODIES" Sandra Norris

I grew up in West Chicago, Illinois. My mom left when I was 4 years old. She took everything in the house including our clothes. My sisters played with dolls, but my dad taught me how to weld, I had a mini bike, a go cart and tractors. We would go to junk yards every Saturday and do odd jobs for extra money.

I am a USAF veteran, and was raped by my superior while I was in a military Tec School. Doctors diagnosed that I have PTSD and severe depression because of it.

I've had a drapery business for eight years and have been an interior designer for 14 years, a loan officer, and a mortgage broker. I have had two failed marriages and have been the victim of domestic violence. I have abused drugs and became a cocaine user. I would binge when things get difficult for me. I would disappear and get high. I've had it all. Nice homes, BMW's, even after I was divorced, I bought my own home where I lived with my children. I worked at Mt. Vernor Carpet Center in Washington, the best job I ever had.

I moved with my daughter to Colorado where my whole world fell apart. I've had three major car accidents. In 2005, I had two head injuries. In 2006, I was in a coma and life long breathing problems started. In 2007, my ankle and foot came off. I was in a cast for seven months, no standing on it at all. They took me to Rocky Mountain Regional Trauma Center and just assumed I was drinking.

In February 2008, I decided to steal a 9 mm hand gun off of my daughter's roommate's bed. I was going to commit suicide. I got pulled over for not using my turn signal. Meanwhile, my daughter called police and said, "My mom has a gun and was going to kill herself."

I was given a roadside test and was very hysterical. I was handcuffed and placed in the back of the car. I had hid the gun in the car so they didn't know I had it. They were taking me in for DUI. I felt like I was in the Twilight Zone.

I am here at ACDF for violation of probation. My original charge was DUI and unlawful possession of gun. Before I violated probation, I joined metro church and I was clean for 16 months.

While my father was nearing the end of his life, I relapsed on cocaine. I used it for a few weeks. I was devastated, both for the relapse and for watching my dad die. I missed classes and had hot UAs. My counselor was heart broken, not to mention God who already knew. I tried to commit suicide by taking 40 30 mg Tomazapam pills and woke up two and a half days later. Talking to my psychiatrist, I should have died. God has a plan for me. There are numerous other occasions I should have died, but by His amazing grace I am still here.

My father passed away July 23, 2009, from a severe case of cancer, after they amputated his leg on February 08, 2009. I realized it's the relationships that you build in this life that count, not material things. I had lost the most important man in my life. I worshipped the ground he walked on. I read him his last rights on July 22, 2009, and told him to go get some of grandma's sugar cookies for his job well done here. Take that magic carpet ride up to Jesus. See you later. He passed away the next morning. He was 71 when he passed and had only one leg.

Once released from our earthly bodies we get our heavenly new ones. My father got his leg back. He was renewed.

"But those who hope in the LORD will renew their strength. They will soar on wings like eagles; they will run and not grow weary, they will walk and not be faint." (Isaiah 40:31) "And I heard a loud voice from the throne saying, 'Now the dwelling of God is with men, and he will live with them. They will be his people, and God himself will be with them and be their God. He will wipe every tear from their eyes. There will be no more death or mourning or crying or pain, for the old order of things has passed away.' He who was seated on the throne said, 'I am making everything new!' Then he said, 'Write this down, for these words are trustworthy and true.'" (Revelation 21:3-5)

Prayer: "Dear Lord Jesus, I ask for your forgiveness; to pardon me, to help me so I no longer blame or am angry with someone who has done me wrong. Please forgive me for I know what I have done and I fall short every day. Help me to know that you and you alone are the only one who won't forsake me. The Scripture says, '*I will never leave you nor forsake you.*' (*Joshua 1:5b*) Please Lord, fill me with the Holy Spirit so that I may learn to obey your commandments. Amen."

Chapter 9

Tornado of Accidental Death

1. "THE LESSONS I LEARNED" by Robert Garcia

In September and October of 2010, I was charged with DUI's. I always thought of myself as a social drinker. The problem is everyone that drinks in excess is fooled by the devil who makes us think that way. The law is specific on what your blood alcohol content should be, to be a legal driver. It doesn't matter what your tolerance to alcohol is.

In 2001 my first wife was riding her bicycle at 7:00 p.m. Her purpose was to get some exercise in the early evening; she was hit and dragged 150 yards by a drunk driver. She was killed instantly. The biggest mistake I made is that I did not take this as a message from God to change my way of life.

In September and October of 2010, I was charged with DUIs. My court on both cases were pending. After deep depression had set in my current wife and I decided to see my good friend, Robert, in Arizona. The second day we were there we saw the sights by riding motorcycles. After riding around for about three hours we started heading back toward my friends' home. As we were going down the highway, a drunk driver ran a stop sign and killed my friend in front of me with his truck. I had a skull fracture and 50% loss of vision in my left eye. My wife had minor scrapes. However, she had the task of attending to everyone laying on the ground in pools of blood. Two flight for life helicopters came, one for Robert and one for his niece who ended up having brain surgery. Robert died before making it to the hospital. My first wife and Robert's death were distinct messages from God for me to change my life.

After being involved in these tragedies, I vowed that I would not simply "control" my drinking, but rather that I would quit drinking completely. I would not let the devil have the opportunity to inflict his temptation in me to drink ever again. It has taken me a long time to get over Robert's death. I truly loved him like a brother. My first wife and I had already been divorced when the accident happened. It was heartbreaking to watch my two sons go through the mourning process.

After going through the tragedy, I had to face the judge on my charges back home. I received 60 days on my first offense and one year on my second, with no option of work release. In my youth I had two priors which justified the one year.

I did a lot of soul searching while being in custody. I knew I had to change my ways and walk with God. *"The LORD is close to the brokenhearted and saves those who are crushed in spirit." (Psalm 34:18)*

It's easy to have remorse while in custody. There are no outside temptations to do otherwise. The real test is to serve God every day of our life. The seed of the Holy Spirit was planted in me at an early age. As I grew older, my direction in life was not that of religion. God has a plan for everyone. He uses problems to draw us closer to Him. We learn things about God when we suffer that we cannot learn any other way. I have developed a hunger for the Holy Spirit. My faith gets stronger every day. God has already blessed me by reversing the judge's decision and granting me work release. We have a minister in our pod with a master's degree in theology who leads us through Bible study every night. He is leaving us soon and has asked me to take his place. *"In his heart a man plans his course, but the LORD determines his steps." (Proverbs 16:9)*

2. "THE ANSWER" by Mireya Vizcarra

Today, May 30, 2011, nearly 23 years have passed since my tragedy. At a very young age, I had the most terrible and painful experience of my life. I suffered both physical and mental abuse from the same man who would later get me pregnant. My pregnancy gave me the strength and courage to get away from him. I was in a place unknown to me and away from my family. I had been living in California for 23 years.

I gave birth to a baby girl. She made me feel proud about myself and was the reason why I wanted to keep moving forward in my life. My mother and sisters came from Mexico to welcome the new member of our family. Their hearts were full of love for my daughter. Two months after she was born, we were on our way to our first vacation in Mexico (my daughter, mother, sister and a cousin). We went on this trip and were very excited. I was driving.

My daughter was next to me and my mother was holding her. While I was passing through a little town between 5:00 a.m. and 6:00 a.m., I had an experience that I had never felt before. I felt like we were in a heavenly place, floating. Everybody was sleeping but my daughter and me. We were looking at each other, eye to eye. I never thought that would be my last time seeing her eyes open. She probably wanted to tell me that she would miss me and that she loved me, too.

Soon after I fell asleep, what felt like just a few seconds, all of a sudden I woke up, it was too late. Oh no! What happened next was horrible. I was trying to control my car which was already out of control. I have no idea how many times the car rolled over. When it stopped, the car was on top of me on the highway. People stopped to help us. I was fully conscious and concerned for my baby. I cried, "Please find my baby! Look for her! I am okay."

They were digging a hole so my body would not suffer the pressure of the car. Why me? How? I couldn't believe all this was happening to me. I was in indescribable pain. Help arrived. My daughter and my mother were the first to be transported to a hospital by helicopter. My sister, cousin and I were transported to the hospital by ambulance.

My daughter was dead. My mother was in a coma, with only a 20% chance of survival. If she did survive she might be in a vegetative state or mentally ill. I was angry at God and asked, "If you really exist, why is this happening? Why am I alive?

Why did I survive? Why am I not dead? That way I would not be feeling this horrible pain. Why? My daughter was the only reason for me to fight for life. She was taken from my arms." My suffering, grieving and pain wasn't enough. This was my fault. I am guilty. I was the driver. I killed my own daughter.

After three months, my mother responded. She was disabled, having suffered enough brain damage not to be normal ever again. Since then my anger was like a seed in my heart, growing. I didn't realize that the anger was covering my pain and tears. My personality and my character was changed overnight. I would not tolerate mistakes or wrong from anyone. I was hiding my grief, pain and anger. Focusing on succeeding in life, working many hours, and exhausting my mind and body.

My mother suffered for more than 18 years after the accident. When she passed away my anger grew. I didn't talk to any of my sisters anymore. Two and a half years passed by and I started reading a Catholic Bible; the Bible started to open my eyes and my heart. I asked God many questions. My understanding of Jesus' love, his life and his suffering was my breaking point.

Today He answered the questions that I had been asking Him 23 years ago. Why did I survive? Why was I alive? Why didn't I die in that accident? With a very loud, calm, kind and soft voice, He spoke to me. He had a purpose for me. His will for me in life wasn't done. He definitely wants me to tell others that He loves us, He forgives us and to forgive every single one that hurts us or has done something wrong to us.

After understanding the real reason of Jesus Christ's crucifixion was to forgive all my sins, I was able to forgive myself and others as well. I started to change. That is when I learned to be humble and to have compassion for myself and others. Forgiving was my master key. Using it helped me to open a door that hindered me from walking to the other side and finding the real me: the person that God wants me to be, with a heart to use to love Him first and then others. I really love Him. I can't stop it. I am in love with God.

"My Daughter, my baby, I always wonder how you are looking at me. You and I had a very short time together and we know how deep those precious moments were. I still miss holding you in my arms. You know I told you to behave very good all the time no matter where we were. It was as if you always understood me. Well until today I miss having you next to me. One day we will be together for eternity. I love you very much and everybody in our family has a beautiful memory of you. They miss you too. We love you very much."

"To my beautiful Mother, You are in my heart and you will always be remembered. I have very beautiful memories of you. You taught me your ways very well. I see myself as a reflection of you. I love you very much. I am comforted to know how happy you are after suffering so much physical and emotional pain while you were on earth. I thank God for giving me understanding of your happiness when I see you in my dreams. Now you are healthy and are smiling and laughing in heaven. I just can't wait to be with you. I know we will have a great time singing and dancing for our King. I love you very much. I miss you even more. Just wait for me. See you soon, dear Mother." Your daughter.

Chapter 10

Tornadoes of Trauma and Betrayal

I was talking with a retired Air Force chaplain who is a good friend of mine. He told me he suffered from what he had seen as a chaplain. Many incidents horrified him to the point that he is traumatized today. He told me if he wrote what he had seen, others would also be traumatized. So, he cannot write what he had experienced. Meeting Kristin Madril helped me understand what he was saying.

I have seen many terrible things while working at a trauma center in the past. I have seen many deaths and injuries, caused by accidents or suicide in both the Emergency Department as well as in the ICU.

One incident I remember is a man who shot himself in the stomach. His abdomen was all patched with clear tape. He was hooked to a machine and the family was frantically trying to find out if he would wake up. His organs were damaged and he had little brain activity.

His family, who was in shock, couldn't see that he might not make it. They were angry at the hospital for not doing anything. They decided to move him to another hospital to see if he could make it. The hospital staff told me he was beyond recovery but his family couldn't accept it.

Another thing I remember is when I was called to see a patient, I found a woman whose body looked like it had been eaten by something. All of her body was rotted away and she was in a coma. I couldn't believe what I saw. I felt like I had seen hell when I saw her. When the family asked me to pray for her, I went up to her and started reading the Scriptures. Then I saw tears rolling down her cheeks. She was considered to be in a coma, but she understood what I was reading. My hospital chaplaincy taught me a lot, but this is one incident that I will never forget. How can a person survive with wounds like that all over her body?

I also have seen doctors opening the heart of a person in the Intensive Care Unit and a nurse was massaging the heart to make the heart beat because the family was frantically asking them to do everything to bring the man back. I asked the doctor if anyone recovered from this stage. He didn't say anything. I could tell that the doctor was only doing this to make the family happy.

Eventually, the man died. The medical team prolonged the suffering of the man, because the family was not ready to let him go. I have grieved, sometimes for days, from the shock of what I heard or saw in the hospital. Similarly, I have grieved from the tornado stories told by inmates I've encountered while ministering to them.

But So far the terrible condition of people and what I have heard from others, cannot compare to what I have heard from Kristin. I asked her to write her story by using the TLT model. After I read her story, I was shaken for two days. I couldn't believe what she had gone through. I couldn't believe what people can do to create hell in other people's lives. I knew when others would read her story, many would be traumatized as well.

This experience helped me to understand what the other chaplain was talking about. He knows that his writing can be horrific and that others would be traumatized.

I met with Kristin and explained that her story could traumatize others. I asked Mary who was in the same pod to help Kristin to rewrite it, omitting all the details of her experience. I told them the purpose of writing her story was not to traumatize others, but to tell the story of how she was processing her trauma with God's help so others can learn from her; how they, too, can process their traumatic experiences.

Mary helped Kristin rewrite the story. Here is her story.

"I PRAY FOR MERCY" by Kristin Madril

By the age of six, I had been influenced by people in the

Pagan religion. I started cutting myself at age 13 and by the time I was 16, I had become a Satanist and was shooting heroin. I was extremely addicted, out of control, living on the streets, and into gangs.

In 1997, the day before Mother's Day, I was invited to a party at an abandoned house by a boy I used to be involved with. I was only 17 years old and didn't think anything of it because I thought I could trust my homies. When we walked in they handed me a drink already made and I drank it.

Shortly afterward my vision blurred and I fell to the ground. Eight guys began to rape me, one after the other. The next thing I remember is someone stomping my face and head in. Then I heard someone say, "I told you we would get her."

I remember praying to God and telling Him that I was sorry for whatever I had done. At this point, God was not a big part of my life. I felt that in just a matter of time I would be dead, so I prayed and prayed for God to hear my cry.

Within 24 hours of my brutal rape, I was rolled out onto Interstate 25. I was left for dead with my body all bloody and battered. I thank the Lord that a woman stopped for me and called 911. I was taken to North Suburban Hospital and put on life support. My mother was in shock when she received the phone call to come see me.

After a couple days on life support I woke up to my family crying and asking, "Who did this?" I was so angry and wanted to handle this myself; I didn't want to give an answer. When they explained the damage done to my body I could only thank God that I was still alive. They found numerous drugs in my system, including GHB, known as the date rape drug, which immobilized my body throughout my experience. They also found on my body feces, urine, boot marks, blood and glass. Inside my body they found glass and semen. I was open from my rectum to my vagina.

Thank God again that the lady who found me and called 911 had copied the license plate number from the vehicle that rolled me out onto the highway. It was then that I told who it was, but I was scared and didn't want to press charges.

Three weeks later I was able to see again and left the hospital with nothing but revenge on my mind. I heard that the guys were arrested but let go because they were minors. At this time, all I could think was God had other plans for them.

One year later, I found out that two of those guys had committed suicide, and four of them were looking at prison time but were nowhere to be found. The last two got off the charges scott free.

Today I suffer from Post Traumatic Stress Disorder (PTSD) and hear voices telling me how dirty I am and that I should hate myself. I have nightmares all of the time of being raped or murdered. Because of the horrific experience I lived through, I take medications.

On February 23, 2000, I overdosed. I mixed three different drugs at one time, which should have been enough to finish me off. My Dad didn't know what to do because he was strung out, too. So he called my sister and told her I was dying.

At this time I thought I was dead, already gone. All I could see was darkness. I thought I was going to hell. It was dark, cold and empty. I saw demons, and one had his hand held out for me to grab. As I was about to give him my hand, I heard the most calming and gentle voice, a man's voice. It was just beautiful, and all he said was, "Make your choice." I pulled my hand back and turned around with my eyes closed. I put my arms out and said, "Please don't leave me." Everything went calm. My soul felt weird, but comforted.

When all of this happened, my family brought in a priest to read the sacrament of the sick. I remember feeling mad at them but I was okay, God had me. After three weeks on life support, I woke up and started a brand new life with God. I had to relearn how to read and write.

I gave my life to God after this experience and my story was published in the book, *Maximum Saints Make No Little Plans*. I began my journey of forgiveness in myself and others. I learned that to be who you are is not a bad thing.

I am a strong woman today because I can speak out to others. I was able to forgive wholeheartedly by the power of Jesus Christ because I don't want to die knowing that I am in sin. I turned my life over to God, and with that comes forgiveness. So yes, I forgive all eight of these men and pray for mercy on their souls.

To those who have been hurt by others, to experience healing, start by accepting the fact that it happened. It's not your fault no matter what. I know some say it doesn't work, but my therapy helped me years later to come to grips with my rape.

I like *1 Corinthians 13:1-13* because I never thought I would be able to be loved after this or to love again, but this taught me that love is not judgmental or ugly, but beautiful, just like me. I am in recovery.

God helped me to be strong in faith knowing that He does have a plan for me. I know that it affected me in an awesome way. You would think that my hate and anger would overpower me, but in the end it is forgiveness that has risen above.

In 2010, I can say this, "Thank you Jesus for your love and forgiveness. God, have mercy on their souls, everyone makes mistakes. This takes a big burden off my back to be able to forgive. Amen."

Now, years later and eight surgeries later, I'm back to my bubbly old self. Forgiveness, ladies and gentlemen, there is nothing else like it.

"If I speak in the tongues of men and of angels, but have not love, I am only a resounding gong or a clanging cymbal. If I have the gift of prophecy and can fathom all mysteries and all knowledge, and if I have a faith that can move mountains, but have not love, I am nothing. If I give all I possess to the poor and surrender my body to the flames, but have not love, I gain nothing. Love is patient, love is kind. It does not envy, it does not boast, it is not proud. It is not rude, it is not self-seeking, it is not easily angered, it keeps no record of wrongs. Love does not delight in evil but rejoices with the truth. It always

protects, always trusts, always hopes, always perseveres. Love never fails. But where there are prophecies, they will cease; where there are tongues, they will be stilled; where there is knowledge, it will pass away. For we know in part and we prophesy in part, but when perfection comes, the imperfect disappears. When I was a child, I talked like a child, I thought like a child, I reasoned like a child. When I became a man, I put childish ways behind me. Now we see but a poor reflection as in a mirror; then we shall see face to face. Now I know in part; then I shall know fully, even as I am fully known. And now these three remain: faith, hope and love. But the greatest of these is love." (1 Corinthians 13:1-13)

Chapter 11

Tornado of Homicide

1. "THE LESSONS" by Donna Tabor

I was six months old when my mom was taken. I was there when it happened. My uncle killed my mother with a brick and there was blood everywhere. They tried to save her life but it was too late. My grandparents tried to raise us. Out of nine of us, I am the youngest. When I was one year old, I was sent to an orphanage called the Southern Christian Home. All of my siblings were there except my oldest brother. He stayed with my grandparents.

I was molested when I was seven years old, but no one believed me. I tried to tell, but no one would listen to me. When the people that raised me stopped working at the orphanage, I was devastated. I was 13 years old when that happened and I started to hate the world. I started getting high to kill the pain in my heart. I didn't want to think about what I had to do. I started abusing my body with drugs. I would sell my body for them; I went to jail when I was 15 years old. I thought that was love. I knew about Jesus and God but I really didn't know much about faith or having a relationship with God.

The lesson that I had to learn was that I had to let go and let God work in my life. Jesus started talking to me. But I was saying, "Who are you? How can I trust you? I have never trusted in you." He spoke to my heart. "I am not like any other man. I love you, Donna. I made you. I formed you in your mother's womb. I died for you." At that moment, I was filled with the Holy Spirit and fire. I was 22 years old and praying in tongues. Jesus touched my heart.

I do thank God for my life. I know He has a plan for me. The Scripture says, *"'For I know the plans I have for you,' declares the LORD, 'plans to prosper you and not to harm you, plans to give you hope and a future.'" (Jeremiah 29:11)*

How was I able to forgive my uncle that killed my mother? Again, the Holy Spirit started speaking to me, "How can I forgive you if you cannot forgive?" I had to let go and let God take control. My brother was in prison at the time. I went to see him and my uncle was at the same prison my brother was at. We sat at the table to see each other. My uncle was sitting at the table also and that's when the Lord spoke to me, "Now is the time." I started talking to him. He could not say anything. All he could do was look. It was time for the visiting to be over. We could take pictures before we left.

When it was time to say our good-byes, I walked over to my uncle and gave him a hug good-bye. At that moment in my heart I said to myself and God, "Jesus, I forgave him." I felt free in my heart. It has been very hard growing up knowing I would not see or talk to my mother. But the Holy Spirit, my comforter, started talking to my heart. I heard the Lord Jesus speak to me. He said, "You will see her." I was doing drugs to kill the pain. I do find peace with Jesus. He is everything I need and more. Jesus is my Mother and my Father and my friend. Jesus, He is all and He is number one. He is that great. One of my favorite verses in the Bible is *Psalm 91:11: "For he will command his angels concerning you to guard you in all your ways." "I lift up my eyes to the hills — where does my help come from?" (Psalm 121:1)*

My regret about being a parent was, here I am having children when I was 18 years old. I have three wonderful children. I put two of them up for adoption when they were four and five years old. I had to give them to Jesus. I could not do it any more. I got tired of dragging them here and there. They saw me being abused. It has been a long journey.

I know God can do anything. 14 years later I saw them for the first time, and, oh, what a joy. God can do miracles. He does miracles everyday if you only believe. I kept believing I would see them someday. I kept having faith. My 21 year old daughter has a son. I am a proud grandmother. My son is doing well. We still have to work on some things. In time Jesus will work it all out. I also have a nine year old, and she does not know me. My relatives have raised her. I put my children in the Lord's hands and I know they are safe. *"I can do everything through him who gives me strength."* (Philippians 4:13) *"But seek first his kingdom and his righteousness, and all these things will be given to you as well."* (Matthew 6:33)

I believe in a God who has a great plan for me. It has been very hard to grow up without my mother.

Jesus tells me she is my great angel watching over me. I want to tell my mother "thank you mom for having me." I know God doesn't make junk and I thank you Jesus for my life. I had a vision of Jesus and I do forgive my uncle. While I was writing this, I also had a vision of my mother flowing like an angel in the heavens.

Prayer: "Dear God, Jesus, I want to thank you so much for taking my mother into your arms. Thank you Jesus for loving me; holding me and taking care of me. Jesus, thank you for dying on the cross for my sins. Thank you for washing me clean in your blood. Jesus, I love you. My daddy Jesus, you are everything to me."

2. "FORGIVENESS" by Nedra Walker

I had thought for a long while that the death penalty was wrong. Four and a half years ago that belief was challenged when my son Jeff was murdered. He was 45 years old and at that time was not living entirely by his belief in Christ. Jeff was our much loved third son. He was born when Mike was three and Stan was 17 months old. I was 21 and his dad was 23. He was a beautiful baby and stayed that way his entire life.

He loved his family and his animals. At about age 16 he dabbled in smoking pot and got into some trouble with the law. He was caught, but continued doing it after a shot with probation. Jeff became more and more rebellious until the age of 17 or so, and when he straight-armed his six year old brother going down the hallway of our home, his dad threw him out.

Jeff called me at work to tell me good-bye and left for Pine Bluff, Arkansas, hitch-hiking. He wanted to see his best friend whose family had moved there several months earlier. He had only been there a short time, before he got into some trouble and landed in jail. His friend's mother told him she would bail him out if he would attend church with her family. That was his first real encounter with the Lord.

Jeff later joined the Army and was stationed in Oklahoma for a year. At that time he came to California to visit us while on leave. When his two-week leave was up and he made no move to go back, I questioned him about it, and he was AWOL. He was always honest when he was caught at doing something wrong. We took him to a nearby base to turn himself in and after getting back to Oklahoma, was honorably discharged. He headed back to Pine Bluff where he found a job learning how to paint houses which he continued throughout his life. He also found the girl he wanted to marry. She was a Christian girl and that changed his life again as he wanted to become a Christian too.

They moved to Tyler, Texas after their second child was born, got into business for himself and bought a house. The house was just a shell and he built it into a comfortable home and had another child. Jeff still had a penchant for picking up people off the street and bringing them home to feed and help them while he told them about the Lord. Some continued to hang around as friends and were converted, but others drifted away and just stayed for the free meal.

All of this didn't make his wife very happy, but things went along pretty well for awhile and they had a fourth baby. His wife went into labor and was having a home birth as usual. The mid-wife noted trouble and they rushed her to the hospital. Unfortunately, they couldn't save the baby. Anna was stillborn. This was the beginning of the end of the marriage.

Jeff, instead of turning to God in his grief, turned to drugs, and his wife after a 17 year marriage, filed for divorce. Jeff went to stronger and stronger drugs, and more and more to the kinds of friends that used drugs. He would try to climb out of the life-style for a few months at a time, but the draw of drugs was too strong until that terrible night when he was shot to death because of a drug deal gone bad.

My first thought after the initial grief was why? Why was my other son Erick, who was there, not killed also? At no time did I wish for the killer to be killed. Any revenge I may have felt was that he would be caught so he couldn't kill again. He had killed a man before and after Jeff's death, but they were contract killings. I knew his name and saw his picture from the papers. He plead guilty to avoid the death penalty and received 30 years for each murder to be served concurrently. He was only 24 years old.

My thought was how young he was and I felt bad for him. I also wondered how his family must be feeling about what he had done. From there I tried to put him out of my mind.

My church family gave us all the comfort they could and I thank God for their support. I see now that God's ultimate plan was to heal my heart, and a change started in me a few months later.

Until I attended a retreat for several women in my church, I was a Christian in my head but not in my heart. It was there that in meditation I received a call from Christ to "Come to Him." I was standing on an overlook off the river below. It was quite a distance down and I had always been afraid of heights. But I was standing there and Christ was standing on the other side across the ravine. He held out His hands and said, "Come to me." I was unable to move because I was afraid, but Christ kept advancing and repeating "Come to me" until He came up and touched my hands. At that point He retreated to the middle of the ravine, standing in the air. Again He held out His hands and said, "Come to me" and advanced towards me, and finally, I let go of my fears and went to Him. I surrendered into His loving arms with all abandon and knew I would do whatever He asked me to do. Eventually, I was told by the Holy Spirit to attend classes being held once a week at our church called, "Joy of Living." It was with this study that I learned forgiveness.

It started by the Holy Spirit telling me to write my son's murderer and witness to him. I put that off for quite some time, thinking, "What, me Lord? You've got to be kidding, Lord!" Finally, I called the detective involved in the case to see where the young man was incarcerated and how to send mail to him. Even then I put off writing for a while. I wasn't sure what to say or how he would react. With my studies of the Bible I found others who were murderers; David, Moses, and Paul to name three, and yet God called them to serve Him. Another case against the death penalty and for forgiveness is *2 Peter 3:9-10*, *"The Lord is not slow in keeping his promise, as some understand slowness. He is patient with you, not wanting anyone to perish, but everyone to come to repentance. But the day of the Lord will come like a thief. The heavens will disappear with a roar; the elements will be destroyed by fire, and the earth and everything in it will be laid bare."*

As I watch others, not just that young man needing repentance, I pray they will all have time before Christ's return. Christ also says to love everyone, including those who are enemies, those who persecute you, not just those who love you back. In corresponding with this young man for almost two years, a wonderful thing has happened in us. I have forgiven him and we have become friends who can love each other, talking to each other about lots of things. I hurt for what he has to go through in prison. I would like for all prisoners to have a chance for repentance and a chance to restore their lives in Christ. I feel that all those incarcerated, no matter what their crime, can be rehabilated if shown how. The young man has shown me that's possible. He now witnesses to me as much or more than I witness to him and I am looking forward to meeting him in prison one day in the near future. I would like to hug and say "Hi" as I do with all my friends.

3. "LIFE CHANGED FOREVER" by Mary Smith

I don't like changes and I never have, but my life and the lives of all my family, especially the life of my son, were changed forever in 2007. When I was asked to write a note detailing what I, as a mother, went through emotionally as the minutes, days, hours, and years of this event unfolded, my initial response was "yeah, no problem." But when I began thinking about what to write and how to begin, many old feelings and many hurts resurfaced and I questioned if I had the strength to sift through those memories; they just hurt so much. But the doubt was temporary. I knew that all my pain would mean nothing unless I choose to rise above it and use it to help others. I want to let others know what I have gone through and how I survived.

When I received the call that my son had taken the lives of two people, his next door neighbors, I was beside myself. Words truly cannot capture the emotions I felt. "No! No! It can't be ! Not my son!" I repeated over and over again. "Not my son!" My husband, hearing and seeing my obvious reaction, rushed over and asked me what was wrong. I literally collapsed in a pile beside the phone from the weight of such emotion.

After collecting my thoughts, I immediately called my sister and my best friend for support and prayer. I am a strong believer in the power of prayer and my household has always served the Lord. All I kept asking myself at this point was, "Why? Why is this happening to my son, happening to me, happening to us? Why is this happening to my sweet daughter-in-law who loves my son so very much?" I felt dead inside!

You see, my son has struggled with many severe mental illnesses since the age of fifteen. He has been medicated and psychoanalyzed for more than half of his life; he was even institutionalized at one point. He was seeking treatment up until the day of his crime, and was on disability for severe depression. Some may look at my son and see a murderer. But I look at him and see his pain, I see my hurting son!

Andy's incarceration grieves me like a death would grieve me. I grieve for the life that my son will no longer have with his wife, with his brother, and with me. I grieve for the everyday things that my son will no longer get to enjoy. I grieve for his loss of freedom, and I especially grieve for his mental state. I see my son imprisoned externally, like he has been internally for so long and oh, how I grieve. I grieve for Andy the same way I grieve for the death of another son who was killed in a car wreck sixteen years ago. I know that everyone grieves differently and the length of the process varies from person to person. As for me, I never got over losing one of my sons to a car wreck and I don't think I will ever get over "losing" Andy.

To help me get through the situation, I would read the Bible and any other book or article I could get my hands on that contained something inspirational. I know that the Lord is with us when we grieve, even though we may not feel His presence. I know that I made it through both of these difficult times because He was with me. I would go to work every day, but I was like a zombie. I would cry all the way to work, I would cry at noon, and I would cry all the way home. Sometimes I would wonder if I had any more tears left. I would cook supper and then sit down to watch television and get my mind off of things, but I found that television did anything but get my mind off of things. Everything on television would remind me of crime or the criminal process, so I quit watching television and would instead read and pray.

Every night my husband and I would pray and pray for my son, for the attorneys handling his case, and for the jury. We prayed that the Lord would bring my son peace and strength and that the attorneys and the jury would be led to do what was best for my son. I don't know what I would have done without my husband being so supportive. I could cry on his shoulder anytime. My husband dealt with the situation by finding work outside and keeping himself busy, but I knew he was grieving too, just differently from me.

When my best friend and fellow church member noticed that I was not laughing anymore or wanting to do any of the things I used to like to do, she told our pastor. I had already been seeing a psychiatrist for several weeks when my pastor called. I decided to cancel the psychiatrist as she was not really helping me. I went to see my pastor two times a week for several weeks and then once a week for awhile. My husband went with me several times. My pastor told me that he had a hard time finding the right words to say because my situation was new to him. He had never been through something like this before.

As my pastor, I could tell that he was genuinely concerned and bothered by the whole situation also. I knew that he had prayed before each of our visits because he would give me verses from the Bible that the Lord had laid upon his heart to give. One of them which stuck with me is, *"So do not fear, for I am with you; do not be dismayed, for I am your God. I will strengthen you and help you; I will uphold you with my righteous right hand."* (Isaiah 41:10) I believe that the visits with my pastor helped me to break through the pain and begin my healing. I had my husband, another son, a sister, and my friends and best friend all helping me to get through this trial. I believe that without all of their support I would have gone crazy.

Andy was initially held at the County Jail. All I wanted to do was grab hold of him and give him a big hug! He was and always will be my baby. But I couldn't give him a hug. All I could do is watch helplessly from the other side of the glass. I wanted to tell him that everything would be alright even though I knew that it wouldn't be. My son had several court appearances but I could only attend one of them. It was so hard to see him attached to all those chains. It made me sick to my stomach to see him like that.

My daughter-in-law was so strong through everything. She attended all of the court hearings that she could, which was most of them. I knew that the Lord was with her, giving her strength. One of the most difficult things I had to face was testifying at his trial, but I knew that the strength of the Lord was with me. I had to answer questions about his childhood. I had to answer questions about his history of mental illness. I had to say things in front of my son that no mother wants to say. After my testimony, I went out in the hall and cried. I cried because the realization hit me again that all of this was for my son! I worried that I may have said the wrong thing. I worried I may have made things worse.

I had prayed and prayed that my son would get sent to a mental hospital where he could get the help he needs, but things didn't work out that way. He was sentenced to life without parole. When my husband and I received the call informing us of his sentence, I didn't know how to deal with the intense pain. I felt like I had died a little more inside. I prayed that God would give me the grace to accept His will, even if it was different from mine. I pray serenity prayer: "God grant me the serenity to accept the things I cannot change, courage to change the things I can, and the wisdom to know the difference."

I don't ask God "why?" so often now. Maybe I will find out the answer once I get to heaven. But once I am in Heaven will the answer really matter? I believe that God has a plan for my son despite his difficult circumstances. I am praying that God is going to make something good out of something bad. There are only two ways that people come out of things like this; stronger or bitter. I didn't want to be bitter. I believe that the Lord knows my thoughts even before I do, so I felt I had the freedom to talk out loud to Him and tell Him how I really felt; even if it was anger. At times I accept the outcome of the trial, but at other times I bawl like a baby. I am still struggling to find peace with this situation, and sometimes fear that I never will. I find that at times I blame myself. I question if I did something wrong as a mother. I fear that I deserve all of this. I feel guilty. Sometimes our circumstances don't change when we pray. Sometimes we are changed.

Now when I visit Andy in prison, I get to hug him. The first visit was hard. Every visit is hard. I try my best to make the visits pleasant for both of us. To see him there, caged and severely depressed is too much for me. I still cry on my way home. This has been a very difficult time in my life, though through it I have gained a revitalized interest in the Lord and a hunger to know Him better personally. I told my son that this should be our verse.

"And we know that in all things God works for the good of those who love him, who have been called according to his purpose." (Romans 8:28)

Not much has changed in the last 4 ½ years of my life since my son, Andy, was sentenced to life in prison. I really rely on the Lord and His grace to get me through each day. The life of my daughter-in-law, however, has changed. After 4 ½ years with no real future with him, with Andy missing from her daily life, she finally decided to divorce him. She still loves him, still goes to the prison and see him, and said that signing the divorce papers hurt her. I love her like a daughter, so I asked the Lord for help getting through yet another of life's storms.

During the time when my son was in jail, court appearances and the trial I quit teaching junior church, which I love being around the children. I couldn't concentrate on studying and in a way didn't feel like I should be teaching children. Now with the Lord's help, prayers from my family, friends and church family I'm back taking my turn teaching junior church and being around the children.

For my son, the first six months in prison was a very hard adjustment for him. All he would do was go for his meals, and the rest of the time he would sleep the day away. He didn't take showers, shave, brush his teeth, etc. What we heard was his cell-mates got tired of him not cleaning up. The psychologist on duty in the prison put in a request for Andy to be taken to Pueblo prison psych ward. She later told him that she was getting worried about him, worried he would have done something to himself. He was there for six months and put on the drug Abilify.

Since he has been back to the prison he is a changed man. He is like he was years ago, good to be around. Andy gives all of the credit to the Lord for him being sent to Pueblo and getting on the right medicine. It is so great to talk to him and visit with him on the phone and in person when we get a chance to visit with him. We now know we can reason with him. It makes me feel as if he has accepted his life is in prison, and that we can keep on making our lives normal, so we can be here for him.

Much like a book I read "A New Kind of Normal" I feel that is my life now. When I have tried to take my life over, it does not turn out like I think that it should. But, when I give my storm to the Lord, my life goes better. God is Good!

Chapter 12

Tornadoes of Abuse and Addiction

1. "SOUL SEARCHING" by Dee Anderson

I have walked down many paths and traveled many roads; most of the time feeling I was in this alone, but today I am here with God by my side to share my testimony. This is my story...seven kids, a mother, no father, no guidance, no love, no structure and no home. Drugs, violence, and abuse was the only normality we had in our lives. My mother was a heroin addict, and she loved cocaine too, slamming it, snorting it, and in turn she ended up smoking crack too. She was a raging alcoholic as well.

It was scary enough to see her drinking or bumping a line, but it was terrifying seeing her tie off her arm and slam a load into her veins. Just a child who's innocence had been taken because my mother needed her next fix. She never had the money so she would sell me to men in exchange for her drugs. I got molested and raped starting at the age of three. I constantly lived in fear. Somehow I always ended back up with my mother.

I was the head of household pretty much. I was taking care of my three siblings and my mother (my other three siblings had not yet been born). I fed them, clothed them and found us places to stay. Sometimes it was just in an abandoned car, but it was better than on the street directly. I would just want to cry and close my eyes in hopes this would all go away but I knew it wouldn't. Sadly this was my reality.

One day my mother was in a rage and I knew it wouldn't be good. She told me to go get her the gallon of vodka off the table. I refused because I told her drinking was bad. She then got up in a rage, got it herself and said, "Why you got to make everything so difficult?" I told her I would never drink and I think she should quit drinking, so she pinned me down, knees on my chest, with all her weight on me and one hand plugging my nose forcing me to open my mouth for air. She forced that gallon of vodka down my throat. I tried not to swallow but when I'd gasp for air, I swallowed. Then after it was gone, she hit me on the head with it, and cracked my head open.

I finally ended up in the hospital and child services got called. I got taken away and me and my siblings got separated. We ended up in foster homes, shelters and group homes. Somehow, we always ended up right back with our mother. The foster homes weren't any better. I continued to get abused and molested. Each time we ended up back with our mother, she became progressively worse. More abusive with the drugs and more abusive to us kids — me in particular. She abused me mentally, emotionally, sexually and physically. She would shatter glass bottles on my back, she even threw me down the stairs, burned me with her crack pipe, stabbed me, kicked me through a window, broke my leg and arm and foot and collar bone.

She would always tell me how worthless I was and how she wished I would die. Sometimes she would be involved while she let men molest me. She hated me as if I was ruining her life! I was only a child but she didn't care about anything she did or how it would affect me. Due to some things I've endured, I am scarred for life. She was going insane.

All this continued for years. Then one day my aunt decided she was going to take me, my sister and my twin brother and newborn baby sister in. She already had three kids and was a single mother. I thought this was going to be wonderful. When we met her, she seemed really nice like a mother should be. Her kids seemed real nice too! I thought surely this couldn't be true! Everything went well for a honeymoon period.

She took us to church, I learned about God. She got us new clothes, fed us and even read stories to us. She didn't drink or do drugs. She never yelled or abused me. It was wonderful until one day she found out she had to either take guardianship of us or her funding was gonna get cut short. So all this time it was about money! That's when the honeymoon period was over. She became abusive and she would even let her kids hit me. I took the fall for everything and for everyone. I was back to being miserable.

As time passed, I became more and more angry, bitter, and hateful. I started displaying it and was punished for it even worse. I got locked in a room in the basement, the floor was cement. I had no books, no bed, no food, no games, and no clothes. I was naked on a cement floor. This created more resentment. I started fighting and showing my anger. I ended up getting molested again and again.

I would pray but nothing changed. I ended up going back into foster care. I ran away and started gang banging at the young age of ten, but by age ten, I had the mentality of a 20 year old. I got jumped on by my O.G.'s and their sons and passed my initiation process to become accepted in. I used my anger and rage toward violent acts making my way up in my gang very fast. I gained approval, they showed me they were proud of me. They rewarded me. I had a place to stay, I never went hungry and I was always protected.

I thought I finally had it made. Life was better than ever before. I still ended up in foster homes and group homes but my homies were always there. I bounced in and out of juvenile hall but whenever I got out I was always still protected, clothed, fed and housed.

By 12, I had gotten my tattoos for my gang: my marks in. I emptied my first clip at age 9 and by 12, I was doing big things. By 14, I had become a leader. I was respected, feared and powerful. I ran the trap house amongst many other things. Although I never got into the drugs, I sold them. I was robbing people, stealing cars, and doing drive by's. I had become the gang's youngest most powerful member because of my anger, hatred and resentment. I wasn't scared of anyone or anything. I'd go to any limit to get what I wanted. I was very violent and ruthless. I caught a federal case almost at the age of 14. I was under investigation by the F.B.I. and D.E.A. I got sent to C.Y.A. (California Youth Authorities) for almost a year. They confiscated 32 firearms, nearly $100,000 worth of drugs, money, a Lexus and a Cadillac.

I ended up burying 17 people at their funerals by the age of 15. I saw people get stabbed to death, shot, dragged by cars, and beaten to death. Even my very own cousins and uncles. At 16, I went to boot camp, got my G.E.D., passed with almost perfect scores, got emancipated at age 17 and started some college classes. I was still gangbanging and everything, but I wanted better things in my life. I decided I would enlist into the Army. I had to wait a while until I could ship out for basic and A.I.T. because I needed to get some tattoos removed, such as the ones on my neck and hands that represented my gang.

I began studying the Word of God and attending church, not frequently but on occasion. I liked studying the Word of God but I didn't prefer going to church. In my time before shipping off for the military, I did a lot of "soul searching," as you could call it.

I went and found my mother, she was out here in Denver, Colorado — in the meantime I still lived in Los Angeles, California. I came out here and knocked on her door. She answered high and drunk still even after all these years, what a surprise! She took one glance at me and replied with, "Who the hell are you?" I was pretty disturbed by this and was tempted to turn around and walk away since she had no idea even who I was, instead I replied, "I'm your second oldest daughter." She looked at me in disbelief and reached out her arms to hug me. I gave her no response because I didn't know how, or what to respond with. She said, "What's the matter you ain't gonna hug your mommy? You know I love you. Mommy missed my little girl!" I told her I wasn't a little girl any more. I was 18, a grown adult and it was a little too late to be playing the mommy role now. I waited for her my whole life and she never came.

I just told her I came to let her know I forgive her, and I

updated her on my life, my accomplishments, and successes. I asked her some questions and she gave me no answers and made excuses for what she had done.

I went back home to California. I then soon went to South Carolina at Ft. Jackson also known as "relaxing Jackson." I completed my basic training—an 11 week program. I did my A.I.T. training as well in Ft. Jackson. That was a 42 week program. I completed that as well. Top of my class, top of my platoon and squadron.

I got a full-ride basketball scholarship to Sheridan College, so I decided to start attending college again. I played for two seasons and went back home to California on one of our off season breaks. Never expected what would come next.

I ended up getting kidnapped with my twin brother. We got bound to chairs sitting, facing each other. Some members of the connect with the Mafioso and MS-13's had kidnapped us all because my mother owed thousands of dollars for all the drugs that she used.

They murdered my brother right in front of me. I tried to stop them but I was tied up so I could only do so much. They shot me in my knee, and stabbed me in my thigh above my knee, they shot me in my foot, and stabbed me in my arm. I was in agonizing pain and to top it off they murdered my twin brother right in front of me; his blood spattered on me. They left me to die with him. I was found by members of my click and taken to the Emergency Room. I had numerous surgeries. I lost my scholarship and got discharged from the Army.

My life was falling apart again. I prayed and God told me I needed to stay strong; that wasn't something I thought I could do. I endured so much I was exhausted. My mother never showed up to her own son's funeral. This was all her fault. I wanted to hate her but I soon found out she had H.I.V. and Hepatitis C from all the intravenous drug use.

I came from Los Angeles, California to Colorado once a month for a year to visit her and make sure she was doing okay. Sometimes she wouldn't even answer the door. She was so busy getting high. All I could do was pray for her. I ended up moving to Colorado because God called me to witness to my mother and try to continue to restore our relationship, or at least build one with her since we didn't have one to restore, so I did.

I ended up getting sick with spinal meningitis. I was told I had 24-48 hours to live. I prayed to God to let me die. I was so hurt and lonely and tired of suffering. I was ready to go because I was tired of fighting the battle everyday just to be able to live.

I had a spiritual awakening though, God told me I had a purpose on this earth and in this life. I suffered for over three months in Intensive Care Unit (ICU) fighting for my life. I ended up with a bleeding ulcer from all the drugs and medicine they were giving me; it tore a hole in my stomach lining causing me to bleed internally. I was throwing up massive amounts of blood. I then had to get a blood transfusion from all the blood I had lost. I had to completely rehabilitate myself because I couldn't function. Meningitis destroys your brain and spinal cord so much it shuts down your nervous system, you can't walk, eat, talk or function. It was awful but I did it. I prayed and prayed that God would help me see through this and that He would give me strength to persevere and I did. God is an awesome God.

My grandmother then passed away on my 20th birthday from breast cancer. My mother didn't attend her funeral—her own mother's funeral! I dropped to my knees and asked God, "Why?" I continued to struggle and became depressed. I ended up getting betrayed and lost everything. I started questioning everything.

I caught another few serious charges in ACDF and bonded out in March 2011 but ended up back here in ACDF. I'm facing 10 to 16 years in prison but I started praying day and night again. God has spoken to me in many ways. I have found answers to questions I never dared to ask. I have found strength at my weakest times and happiness in the most miserable place. I finally figured out through God and many others like the chaplain, that God is using me to share my testimony to help others persevere, and become stronger in their faith. The most important lesson I've learned is to let go and trust God; through Him, all things are possible.

2. SEARCHING FOR LOVE — Richard Schmittel

I was born in Freeport, Texas. Strangely enough I was born on a prison farm in Bazoria County. The prison was the Cleman's units. My father worked for the prison system though I've never known what he did. Now 45 years later, the same system I was born into, says I will die in it.

Our family stayed in Texas until I was three years old. I also had three brothers and two sisters. I was the middle child. We moved to Illinois, I presume, to be closer to my mother's side of the family. Being so young at the time, I was unaware of the problems between my parents. I grew up thinking that there was nothing wrong with my dad never coming home. Mom was always there with my brothers and sisters. I did not realize that we were very poor or what it must have been like for my mom to be alone.

Until I was older, perhaps as early as seven or eight, I witnessed the drinking and the fights, and how they would hit each other and destroy things. I remember watching my mother chase my father with a butcher knife and hearing all the children cry. Oh, how they still haunt my nightmares. I guess I thought every family was like this. My mother would get so drunk that if you did not eat, she would dump the food over your head and then would laugh.

My tears were never comforted. There were never hugs to heal my heart. Was this normal? I thought it was. Sometimes my aunt Betty would drag us along to a Pentecostal church. "Holy Rollers," that's what we called them. Supposedly there was a God that loved us. I never saw Him. I do not remember my dad ever attending a service, however, I do not remember him being at home much either.

My mom would beat us with whatever was handy. Her

favorite was a switch that she cut from a tree and test through the air. We middle kids used to take the brunt of her pain. Was it because we were born and ruined her life, or was she showing us love the only way she knew how?

The older kids left quite early. The younger ones were not quite ready for what would later be their sacrifice to the switch monster. I do not think she meant to cause the cuts, though I remember how much it hurt trying to put pants over my legs. She was hurt inside. I guess it was my way of taking some of her tears away. I believe she once loved us but she hated herself.

We moved a lot back then. I cannot really say I have many pleasant memories except when we lived in Trenton, Illinois. I got to play little league baseball. I played every chance I could. It would take me away from the pain. My parents never watched us play, but I was very good. We even went to a championship and to D.Q. afterwards. Though mostly all the kids had their parents and families to share that moment with them, I knew they were overrated.

My mom would go out. I never knew where she would take my older brother. My sister and I would watch the younger kids. Then one night, mom brought hell home with her. His name was Fred. How I met him was the morning I walked into her room and they laid there naked. I was lost in my feelings. I did not know who he was, but soon I would find out by how he would beat my mother and us children. She always made excuses, and stood up for him. Oh, how I wish she could have loved me like that.

One night, I was woke up by a scream or grunt. I made my way down stairs to what was the scene of the worst beating I have ever seen. I stumbled down the stairs and when I saw my mother, her face was in a puddle of blood and she was gasping for air. He was choking her and I do believe if I would not have entered at that moment, he would have killed her. I screamed for him to stop and to let her go, but this attempt only enraged him.

He forced me to sit and watch the beating until I begged to use the restroom. At that time, I backed out through the screen door and ran until I found a police car. The police knew of us. As we drove home, I could not wait. I knew he would stop the beatings now. The police had me wait in the car as they approached my house.

I remember my house door opening and my mother standing there, the blood gone. Why could they not see it? How was this happening? The officers said my mom had no idea of what I was talking about. I was outside and nothing was wrong. "Please do not make me go into that house," I begged. The officers said, "You have to son." As the door closed. I was beat with a switch that night and forced into the basement. I cried myself to sleep but I knew in my heart at least for that night, the beating of my mother had stopped. To this day I still do not understand, only God does.

By the age of 13, I had started using alcohol and drugs. I was given methamphetamines (speed). I found out one of my mother's secrets. Oh, the beatings they never stopped, but because of the drugs and alcohol the pain did not hurt as bad. Sometimes I would not even cry. I knew God was watching and I would not let him see me cry. If He hated me, I could hate Him right back. I felt I had already seen the worst and at the age of 14, I felt I was already in hell. So, I ran and ran. I never stopped. I did however find my so called father in Colorado. He drank and did drugs and I was allowed to do them with him. He really did not care if I was there or not. I was allowed to drop out of school in the 8th grade.

I was not getting beatings any longer, but a different abuse soon started. Though I guess it was his way of loving me, I had about all of his love I could handle. I would sleep at an all night pool hall. The owner Phil knew somewhat about the life I was blessed with so he would allow me to sleep on a back bench. I began selling pot and other drugs so I could eat and face life and get through another day of hell. It seemed to me that God had decided to leave me alone. So, in turn, I left Him alone. I was living for the world, but I always wanted to find love.

Before I came to love my Father God, I witnessed certain things. My uncle C shot and killed his wife one night. Also, my aunt S killed her husband with a shotgun when he slept. She ended up being put in a mental hospital. It seemed to me that our family for some reason was cursed. I pretty much had realized by the time I was 14 or 15 that pain and sadness was a way of life, one that I got used to. The drugs would allow me to escape reality.

Life was not bad as long as I did not have to face it. I still never had anything that resembled love, though my heart so badly cried out for it. I would be at a department store and would see kids my age with families, their dad's arms around them or walking with their moms. I wondered what they thought about me, long hair, patchy pants and army jacket. I pictured myself in their place. Sometimes the tears would force me to walk away. I ran away again to Utah and then back to Colorado.

After three months, my father allowed me to stay with him and at the age of 15, when he would pass out, I would steal his car. That ended one night when I got pulled over. The police took me home, and after seeing my dad drunk and stumbling to the door, the officer asked me, "Are you going to be okay, son?"

I did not realize all along that God had a plan for me. I can't believe I spent years fighting His will. All the deeds of this world that I lived for, my fleshly desires, lust, anger, wrath, my sinful nature continued in my life. My heart was dead and everything I did in the darkness, God was going to bring me to the light.

By the time I was 18 years old, I was headed to prison. The life I led, the path I walked, only leads to death. While this was going on in my life, my younger brother was the one getting beat by my mother and her monster from hell. Chris got a bow, then shot and killed Fred. He was 14 years old. Now the beatings really stopped. Perhaps now when the dreams came, they would not be real, but that's not how it ended up.

I spent several years just existing. Life had very little purpose. I was told that I had a Father in Heaven and that He loved me. I thought you can't be right. He was never there either, just like my real father. I was bitter towards God and was scared of His love and forgiveness. I went to Florida where most of my life changed and started to take on a new meaning.

I had already accepted Jesus as my Savior though I had no idea what a life in Christ meant. I did not have any knowledge of His Word, His love or being a child of God. Though I did know that Jesus went to the cross for me, and suffered beyond all I had ever suffered, and by loving me that much had caused rivers of tears to flow from my eyes, and from my heart. Now for once I had a Father that would never leave me. I did not seek God's will and I soon found myself as lost as ever for my free will was enticed by my human desires.

I was 23 years old and really doing nothing with my life except to out run the pain and sadness that was always chasing me. Until one afternoon, I walked into a bar called the Eagle's Nest, and there my life would change forever! Behind the bar was the love I never had and that my God would bless my life with. She was 21 years old and like myself had never been loved. If there is someone for everyone, then through my years of searching and loneliness, I had found her.

Love was so new and I had never felt love like that ever in my life. She fulfilled all my hopes and dreams more than anyone. We laughed and loved. We became best friends and inseparable. We fell so deeply in love that our hearts and souls became one and now I knew what a family was like. I never had a family that loved me before I met her, but finally now I had a family that loved me. We had three children together and each time God blessed me with more love than any pain I ever knew, and I forgot about the pain that once was in my life.

Her love made me want to be my best but I found that disappointment would always be right around the corner. Her love never let me down and she tried so hard to make a life and family with my broken heart. Somehow we made it through 23 years together. I saw my children grow up and I was a part of their lives through it all. Now 23 years later, my life or any life worth living came to a crashing end. Through the stumbles and hardships, my wife grew tired of always struggling and somehow I was losing my one and only love. I felt so sick inside, throwing up, and having panic attacks. I could not be alone anymore, not again. I had spent my life finding this love. In all my days and all my nightmares, I only dreamed of a family's love and peace and security. I coached little league teams and saw Brit play softball, birthday parties, dinners just between the two of us. "Why was God taking them away from me?"

I found myself so lost and wandering around in a daze. I begged her to let me come home to her and the kids. I found myself watching death, and it screamed out for me! I could not live without the only love I ever knew. My children, I wanted to hold, and I wanted so badly to be held again. I pictured myself growing up and the pain that my children must be going through. Their father was not there; how could I protect them from the world of hell I once dwelled in.

I was turning into my greatest fear. I was a drunk, I could hear the voices calling from hell and I knew I could not let them hurt my family. They were out to swallow up all the love in my life. I remember calling and calling to reach my wife and the kids and as the hours went by I knew in my heart that something terrible had happened. I was terrified and thought I would find them dead. I was alone and lost. I didn't drive anywhere but yet I found myself running. I could not escape the pain this time. It was overtaking me. I ran through homes and went from car to car but the valley of death would not let go of me.

Finally, the police found me and here I wait. I search for moments on memories of love from the past, then I realize when I go to be with Jesus, this pain and the beatings will finally stop at last. There is only one peace. God says we are all predestined and He knew us before we came from our mother's womb. I feel as though we all have a debt that is owed and payment is due. Sounds like my family was lost to this world before we were even born because of the sins of our fathers or grandfathers or even before.

I do not know how long the curse has been on the Schmittel family, though I know I've watched my father die a horrible death. My mother died an alcoholic in her sleep with a glass of vodka in her hand. My little brother Christopher was killed over drugs and a woman. They shot him three or four times then chopped off his head and hands, and buried him in a pit. When they found him, they only identified him by his tattoos because they never found his head or hands. No one has heard from my little sister Tina in 15 years. I know there are pits in life that swallow you up. My older sister is an alcoholic and drug addict, mostly an alcoholic. She was beat up by everyone she was ever with. The rest of the family who knows and who really cares how they are, is a reminder of the pain and sadness of a life of hell that I came from.

I had almost escaped that life and overcame the curse with my wife and the kids but I guess the debt is not paid. I pray to God it ends here with me and that my children go on to be blessed in all that they do. I do feel at peace knowing my Lord and Savior has forgiven me and has lifted the curse from them. I long to see how my children grow and the path their lives will take and hope, love finds them like it found me. Walking through a doorway, I've walked out that door now. God takes me on another journey, a cross I must bear, a love I must surrender; perhaps it never was mine.

I spent years destroying my family, and all that was dear to me. God first heard my cry, my pleas, and the cry of my repentant heart. I am truly remorseful for my sins and sorry for the desires I once loved. God came to me and the Holy Spirit healed me, cleansed me with the blood of His son Jesus Christ at the cross. That was my new beginning, reborn in Christ.

God came to my heart and calmed my spirit and soul.

He took the pain and lifted my burdens from my heart. The weight of guilt was taken off my back. He gave me peace in the hell I was living in. I felt new and cleansed. God started working through me, a sinner. To share His love and forgiveness with others, I tried to convince God that I was not worthy. God said He had chosen the poor of this world to spread His word and He had chosen me. Because of the love God had showed me, I found I wanted to tell everyone about His love and began to see Gods' hand at work in my life.

I do not yet know how God will heal my family but I know as long as I am faithful and always put Christ first, the curse will end with me, and my children will not be under the cloud of sin. I gladly sacrifice my life for their happiness. What more can a father do? God sacrificed His Son so that whoever would believe in Him would be saved.

So, this life now I live in the flesh is but a vapor. I long to be with my Lord and Savior. I long to be in His arms and feel His heavenly love. The Holy Spirit has lifted me up! Each day I start with Christ for it is this fleshy tent through which I do the Lord's will. He guides me down the narrow path that leads to heaven and the New Jerusalem.

3. GOD'S OWN MEDICINE — Francesca Cayou

"On hearing this, Jesus said, 'It is not the healthy who need a doctor, but the sick. But go and learn what this means: "I desire mercy, not sacrifice." For I have not come to call the righteous, but sinners.'" (Matthew 9:12-13)

This is the Scripture I prayed before I began to write my testimony. To me, it means people who don't have a relationship with God can find His grace by recognizing His voice, when they are sinners.

I was born and raised in Sioux City, Iowa. I was taught both traditional and cultural ways, as well as, Christian ways. I guess you could say I had the best of both worlds.

In 1998, I was saved and baptized by the "Pentecostal" church. My mother-in-law was an evangelist there. She taught me how to read the Bible. She said, "Pray for discernment." Once I did, I understood the Scriptures.

In June 2004, I started working as a Certified Nurses Assistant (CNA). Soon it was mandatory that I work weekends. By September, I was working double shifts. I became independent enough to pay my own expenses. I was doing pretty good.

I was raising my two year old son alone. I had a daycare provider during the week. On the weekends I was struggling to find a babysitter. I was missing a lot of work. I needed a little help. A so-called friend of mine offered to watch my loving toddler. I would pay her. I would leave my son Friday night and pick him up Sunday night. I trusted her. Soon she had a boyfriend and he came to live with her. I met him. He seemed like a decent guy. We found out we had a lot of friends in common. We grew up in the same area of Nebraska. I trusted him also.

In May 2005, my son started showing me disturbing behavior. I thought he was going through terrible two's. He would cry a lot. He would touch himself and suck hard on his bottom lip. I noticed blood stains on his legs streaking down from his rectum to his feet.

I asked my son in the calmest voice I could find, "If anything happened to you, you can tell me." In his two year old mind and part sign language, he described the worst sum of my fears. He was sexually abused by the babysitter's boyfriend.

I went crazy. I pulled my hair out. I cried. I broke things. I lost my mind. Thank God, my brother was there to bring me back to reality and comfort me.

I took my son to the hospital. I made a police report with the Thornton police department. But the babysitter lied for her boyfriend. She said that it was probably someone I knew because it was not her boyfriend. So the police dropped the charges because of my son's age. That man walks free today.

I believed my son because at that age, kids don't know how to lie. The behavior was learned. My son's innocence was taken. His personal life was in shambles. He had been betrayed.

My biggest question was "Why? Why did this happen to my son? Why didn't I recognize what was happening? What makes a person think it's 'okay' to molest a child?"

Now I know I will never find out why. Some people are just sick; mentally sick and morally ill, sick in the head, no morals at all. Predators looking for easy prey, like my son.

I was in shock for a long time. I was numb. I lost trust in all people, especially men. I would not let my son sit on a male's lap. I just didn't know who I could trust anymore. Because of these experiences, I only put my boys in day-care not in-home daycare because they need more monitoring and support.

I got my son in therapy right away. I saw no change in his behaviors. He continued to abuse himself. I took him out of therapy. Big mistake. If you have your child in therapy, do not take them out. As I found out, I was taking my son to the wrong therapist, which was good because he needed a specialist in sexual abuse trauma.

I took the advice from my family to teach my son about good touch and bad touch. I spent a lot of time with him, let him know that he was safe. Hugged him constantly, told him "I love you" everyday. But this wasn't enough.

In June 2005, my husband came back into the picture. He was an important person to my son's life. The babysitter's boyfriend had told my son, "I am your real father." So, when he met his real father, my son was confused about who his real dad was. The bond between them was shaky. Bottom line, my son didn't trust a male presence.

In February 2006 and 2007, I had two more sons exactly one year apart, same hospital, same doctor and nurses. Things at home became more crowded and chaotic. I was overwhelmed. My husband and I would drink at night and we had domestic violence issues. My husband would slap the back of my head, punch my ribs and back. He would push me so I would fall down. Then he would stomp on my legs, feet, hands, and arms. He would kick me in the face and head. I would scream, "Please stop!" I remember my boys crying and watching.

When it was done, I would limp to the bathroom to clean the blood. I didn't like looking in the mirror because in my mind it wasn't me that this was happening to. I would leave my body only coming back to stop the bleeding and assess the damage. I kept it a secret because I wanted my family to stay together.

In June 2009, we became homeless. My husband lost his job. We were staying in a shelter. I found a new apartment. I started working again. Things were looking up and I saw blessings. Then, my younger sons started to tell me that my oldest son, the five-year-old was sexually molesting them at night. I had no idea it was happening. I was upset. I knew I had to do something. I reported it to Child Protection Service. I was court ordered to stay away from my youngest son. I had to do group therapy and classes. The social services told me, "Somewhere I stopped protecting my children."

I was fed up. I was angry. I turned to alcohol and drugs. My husband and I were always fighting. I became depressed. I tried to commit suicide. I was unsuccessful. That changed me. I had defeated death. I was unstoppable.

In December 2010, one night while drinking with my husband, he accused me of cheating and became abusive and violent. I finally fought back. Because of that, I sit here in ACDF looking at a lot of time.

As I reflect on the past six years, I have learned a lot of life lessons, especially that prayer was always a consistent part of my life, but I didn't live a Christian life. I prayed to God to help me finish school so I could become independent, to find a job, to find a daycare and babysitter.

I prayed and gave thanks for the ample income, the blessings of paying for my own apartment, bills, and the means to take care of my son.

The one thing I regret is that I didn't trust my

"intuition." My gut feelings told me "something's not right." I ignored the "visions" of my son being abused. I had a feeling (intuition) that something was wrong. I never would of imagined in a million years that those things were happening to my son. But once I knew they did, I cut those people out of my life and I wanted revenge.

One day while telling my aunt what happened, she said, "You won't have to lift a finger. God will take care of it for you." I believed what she was saying because people like that get themselves caught up.

"For there is nothing hidden that will not be disclosed, and nothing concealed that will not be known or brought out into the open." (Luke 8:17) "And if anyone causes one of these little ones who believe in me to sin, it would be better for him to be thrown into the sea with a large millstone tied around his neck." (Mark 9:42)

"Nothing in all creation is hidden from God's sight Everything is uncovered and laid bare before the eyes of him to whom we must give account." (Hebrews 4:13)

I prayed for my son that he would get the help that he needed. Today, my son lives with my brother. He recently was accepted by the Kemp Foundation for a mentor. For 30 weeks during the next school year, he will meet with a doctor from the metro area. He will help my son with homework, social skills and self-esteem. My son is also seeing a specialist in sexual abuse trauma. She is a great therapist. I thank God for her everyday.

When I share my story, a lot of times what I hear in response is "That happened to me, but no one believed me." Sexual abuse happened to me also, but I never told anyone. I give my sons "congratulations" for telling me, because they were braver than I was. I let my sons know how proud of them I am because a lot of people keep such issues behind closed doors or just "sweep it under the rug."

Ignorance festers abuse. Thus creating more dangerous situations for more children. Producing more pedophiles. Saying it is "okay" for such things to go on. Sexual abuse is not a taboo issue anymore. It is okay to tell. It is okay to accept. It is okay to stop the hurt, pain, shame and guilt. Become an advocate for your children. Don't be afraid of "what people might think of you." Help your children to find the right help they need to start the healing process.

Maybe you have issues about sexual abuse because it happened to you, too. This was the case for myself. Because I never told anyone, I had a lot of anxiety attacks. I would have them at any time. I thought I was going crazy. I had to be put on psych-meds to deal with the depression and anxiety. I can honestly say that the medication has helped because I couldn't do it on my own. I take my mental health and the mental health of my sons very seriously. I don't ignore it.

If sexual abuse is an issue for you, please seek professional help from a priest, pastor, or a close friend or relative. Confide in someone and continuously pray to Jesus to overcome the horrible memories. I have found many people are very understanding toward sexual abuse victims. Ultimately, it is up to us, as parents to break the cycle, take a stand, and protect our children.

I know that God saw everything that has happened to my children and my family. There is a reason for everything whether we know it or not. But God is taking care of things in His own time with His own medicine.

I forgave myself, the babysitter and her boyfriend, my now ex-husband, and everyone else who has ever hurt me. I had to let go and let God take care of my pain because it was tearing me up inside. Love is another medicine that has been good for me. Compassion compels me everyday. This is the main reason I went into the medical field. I like the feeling of knowing that I can help someone who can't help themselves to have a better day."*But the fruit of the Spirit is love, joy, peace, patience, kindness, goodness, faithfulness, gentleness and self-control. Against such things there is no law.*" (Galatians 5:22-23)

Chapter 13

Tornadoes of War

1. "RESTLESS YEARS" by Bob Birx

I spent four years in the Army, ten years in the Air Force, and eight and a half years in the Air National Guard. I retired from the military, but I have never had one bullet or one bomb near me, however, my father's story is different. I will share this on behalf of my father and in deep respect and honor of him and for many others who had similar experiences and served our country.

As I grew up, my father, Edward A. Birx, told me the stories of military life that impacted his life. He was in the Marine Corps for four years, three years in the jungle of war which affected the rest of his life until he died.

The first story is about when he was in the jungles of Central America before World War II. One day his patrol found a missionary who was dying. The natives had stakes on his hands and legs and placed him on top of a colony of ants. The missionary had been there for several days. The ants had eaten their way into his eyes and into his brain, but he was still breathing. The marines felt the only way to end his misery was to put a bullet through his head, so they shot him.

The second story I was told by my siblings, for I was too young to remember and my father never spoke of it. On each New Years Eve for 14 years, my father would be anxious and would go out of his mind. He was restless and something was really troubling him. Many years ago, on New Years Eve in the jungle, as he was in a hut with other marines playing cards, he won a particular hand of poker. As he swept up his winnings, his head was down. Suddenly he found that he was sitting with dead marines, all of their heads were cut off. The natives had come through with machetes (long knife) and cut off everyone's head. When my father placed his head down, they missed him.

Another story he shared with me, was when his unit was holding a village in Nicaragua, the guerrilla were advancing by putting the women and children in front. When given the command, they were forced to fire on everyone. After the fire, he heard a medic saying, "Even though the woman is dead, maybe we can still deliver the child."

When my father returned from the war, it was classified as a conflict, not a war. He didn't get any veterans benefits because of that. Worst of all, civilians threw tomatoes at him here in his own country and called him "war monger." Like many returning veterans he buried all the feelings of guilt, shame and pain and he seldom spoke of it.

Before he passed, my father was in a coma for several months. He was 84 years old. After my mother and I prayed for him, he woke up and opened his eyes and said, "I want to pray with you." As my mother went toward him, he said, "No, I want to pray with Robert."

I prayed that God would either take him or let him wake up, but not to keep him in between. My father passed away. I had spent time with my mother and she shared with me that on his death bed, after more than 50 years of carrying all these weights and memories of horror from the war, my father told her that he thought God was punishing him for the things he had done in war.

I think my father was a man who lived a much harder time than I did. There were moments when I thought he was hard on me, but he was actually being much more gentle than he had been treated. I am at peace because I felt that everything that needed to be said between us had been said and I know God does not punish any man for being in a war they had no control of.

2. "WALK OF FAITH" by Bob Carr

I am 81 years old and live in Loveland, Colorado. I was born in 1930 in Afton, New York. I had a loving and cohesive family. I had one sister, now deceased, one brother five years older than I. I was brought up in a Christian home; my maternal grandfather was a Baptist minister. I attended church regularly and our family was very active in the church. I quit going to church when I became a teenager. I really didn't know God.

My best memory of childhood is good relationships and having dinners together, playing cards together, and driving as a family. My father was a railroader and my mother was a house wife. At the age of 16, I graduated from high school. At 17, they were going to draft me into the Army but I didn't want to join the Army, so I joined the Navy. I never had the money or opportunity for higher education.

In the Navy, for the first ten years, our ship chased Russian submarines out of Long Island Sound, and winters from January to April were spent in the Caribbean. Two of my favorite ports of call were Saint Thomas, Virgin Islands and Havana, Cuba.

The hardest thing about being in the military was being away from home and the worst thing that happened to me was while I was stationed in Da Nang Harbor, Vietnam. For two months, we were swinging around the hook (at anchor) and children would come out in basket boats (reed baskets covered with tar) to bum cigarettes. Crew members would come and drop packs of cigarettes over the side of the ship to the children. During a four hour watch, it was my duty to protect my crewmen.

One girl, probably about three years old, stayed close to the ship but she acted differently than the other children did. I watched her closely over a period of the time; she made her way towards the gangway of the ship. When she reached the foot of the accommodation ladder, I noticed that she had a brick of C-4 (high-explosive) in her hands with a pin in it. Her intent was obviously to destroy the ship and in the process commit suicide. When our eyes met, I had no alternative but to shoot her with a .45 caliber pistol. There were about 300 men on the ship and I had to protect them plus the ship itself.

When I had a chance to review what had happened, I

became emotionally unglued (upset) to the extent that I was relieved of my duties as officer of the deck for the rest of the watch. I was in such shock that I didn't think I could make a rational decision at that point.

I had a knot in my solar plexus because of this. I used alcohol to kill the pain. Usually I was sitting in the ship and firing; normally my killing was long range, but this was different.

However, throughout a 20 year Navy career, they had given me an outstanding technological education even to the point of being able to run the department of Electrical Engineering at Boulder, Colorado University for 22 years following my US Navy retirement. I was very successful at work, but I became an alcoholic because of the pain from the knot. I tried to drink myself to death. I came very close to succeeding when I was about 50 years old. I entered the Day At a Time Unit in Boulder, Memorial Hospital, an A.A. sponsored program. I had tried to quit drinking but was unsuccessful.

I was in a hospital in Boulder, Colorado, in the early 1960's, when the doctor came in, sat down on my bed and told me that I had five to seven days to live. When the doctor left the room, I became emotionally unglued. When I finished sobbing and regained some degree of control, I asked a God that I didn't know, "Please help me." I reconciled with God and I went to sleep. A slow, progressive healing began.

My prayer had been answered. I am thankful that upon my asking Him, He has given me a purpose for my life. That purpose resides in my relationships with people: "people are where it's at." I quit drinking and attended A.A. meetings. I became a sponsor for other alcoholics and have been sober for 30 years. A year later, I gave up smoking.

About 15 years ago, we moved to Fort Lupton where I joined a church and became an active member. There was a ditch road and I walked about three miles a day for exercise in the country. I saw wildlife and it was a pleasant place to walk. I had a life changing experience there. One day I was walking, going north. I was in the right hand tire track, north of the house, when all of a sudden, I became aware of an entity walking along beside me on my left. We walked some distance without saying anything. After I recognized and acknowledged His presence, He said, "Bob, let's continue this journey together." I concurred and we walked a little farther; then this entity disappeared. Peace reigned but there was no excitement; however, the episode will be riveted in my mind forever.

While we lived in Fort Lupton, for the first time I was diagnosed with PTSD by a doctor. I was traumatized by war especially by the incident with the little girl. Once I was in a restaurant and suddenly I heard a big noise, I immediately dove under the table trying to hide from the flashback from the war to find my buddy was under there, too! There was no military help or counseling available or even recognition of how I suffered from the war, even now. After I came back from Vietnam, the public treatment of soldiers was hostile and there was no recognition that I had served my country. I was given a piece of paper when I retired and that was it.

What gives me a thrill is when someone thanks me for serving our country. When my son retired from 20 years of military service, he dedicated his retirement ceremony to me because I never had one. He made me happy and I felt honored.

I still have nightmares about the little girl, and I get up and walk the hallways in the middle of the night. I suffer from flashbacks when I see little girls and relive the experience of seeing the little girl's face. I say, "Lord, please help me." Prayer helps me when I am distressed. My memory of walking with Him in Fort Lupton in the field holds me even now. He is walking with me even though I don't see Him. On my deathbed, God heard my prayer, "Please help me." The doctor didn't think I would last this long. Thirty plus years later, I walk, talk and commune daily with my Lord and Savior. *"The LORD himself goes before you and will be with you; he will never leave you nor forsake you. Do not be afraid; do not be discouraged."* (Deuteronomy 31:8)

Chapter 14

How to Process Grief and Loss

1. Practice TLT model.

Healing from grief is a process, depending on your relationship with the person, and how you learned to deal with different emotions including shock, denial, blame, anger, forgiveness, attachments, regrets, and triggers, etc.

You need to process each emotion and eventually let go of the person if you want to be healed from grief. If you are breaking down with tears and sadness whenever you are reminded of your loss, you are in the tornadoes of grief and loss.

When you suffer from the tornadoes of grief and loss of a loved one, it's easy to become overwhelmed, and be immobilized with pain. Read the Chapter three and follow the TLT (Tornadoes, Lessons, and Teaching) model as soon as possible. Don't wait. Don't ignore the problems. Start it now.

2. Process your grief and healing.

When you are in the grief of a tornado, you are thrown into a grieving house which has many rooms. In order to move on from that house, you need to visit different rooms and process them. Those who have visited all the rooms and experienced healing have lessons to teach us. As long as you are stuck in one room or avoid visiting other rooms, you will be stuck in pain.

Working on your relationship with the Lord is the essential part of this healing, so you have to visit a healing room as often as possible. But there are other rooms that you may or may not have to visit, it depends on the nature of death and your relationship with the person you have lost. Ask the

Lord to give you wisdom to process grief and pain so you won't get stuck in grief. God can bring healing into your heart. The following exercises will help you process your grief and loss.

(1) Prayer brings healing: Pray for 30 minutes everyday for the next 30 days. Speak to God for 15 minutes and listen to God in silence for 15 minutes. When you are grieving, there are many thoughts and attitudes that need to be adjusted and cleansed. Resist any disturbing thoughts so you can listen to God's voice without distraction. Prayer: "Lord Jesus, I am hurting. Please heal my broken heart. Help me so I can experience healing. Guide and direct my path so I can follow you and find peace and joy."

(2) The Word of God brings healing: Read the Bible 30 minutes every day for the next 30 days. Read Job, Psalms, Proverbs, John, and other Scriptures, to understand God's love and His healing power in times of grief and pain.

(3) Praising God brings us healing: We can praise God in any circumstance by focusing on God's grace. God is good, even during the loss of your loved one. Death and loss is a result of living in a fallen, imperfect world with frail bodies. Sometimes our loved one's tragic, sudden death may be caused by people's weaknesses and bad decisions. It's not God's doing. God understands our pain and He is willing to help us. If you are angry with God, because you think that He caused you pain by taking your loved one, you need to work on understanding God's love. When you can accept His love and healing power, you then start down the path to restoration. God is for you, not against you. Jesus said, "*The thief comes only to steal and kill and destroy; I have come that they may have life, and have it to the full.*" (John 10:10)

(4) Know that God has eternal plans: All our family, friends, material things, and our lives are temporary gifts from God. He has plans for a better future for those who believe in Jesus. "*He will wipe every tear from their eyes. There will be no*

more death or mourning or crying or pain, for the old order of things has passed away." (Revelation 21:4) But even now, God doesn't want us to carry a big burden of grief and pain. He wants us to live in peace and Jesus can provide it. The Lord said, *"Come to me, all you who are weary and burdened, and I will give you rest." (Matthew 11:28)*

(5) <u>Ask God to heal you from triggers of grief and pain</u>: You will learn what makes you break down in pain when you lose someone. You may need to put away the items that trigger your grief and pain. However, the reality is anything can be a trigger. The ultimate healing will come from the Lord when you put God first and not the person you have lost. Prayer: "Lord Jesus, thank you for your love. I love you. Please help me focus my heart on you so grieving does not become a distraction between you and me. I ask you to heal me so that I don't suffer from any triggers. Amen."

(6) <u>When you are troubled, ask Jesus to anoint you for healing</u>: Put your hand on your head and pray, "Lord Jesus, I am hurting. Please touch me and heal my troubled mind, heart, soul, and spirit. Holy Spirit, fill my heart with your peace and joy, and bring healing. Heavenly Father, I praise you for helping me in my troubled times."

(7) <u>Write a letter to your loved one</u>: Write a love letter, forgiveness letter, releasing letter, or good-bye letter to your loved one or to yourself.

(8) <u>Let go of your loved one</u>: You have to grieve. It is necessary so that you can experience healing. But, if you decide to grieve for the rest of your life, you will be immobilized by the pain. Your relationship with God will also suffer, because your grieving will become a distraction. You have to let your loved one go, in order to experience healing. Prayer: "Lord Jesus, I am giving you all of my desires, wishes, dreams, regrets, and unforgiving spirit associated with my loved one. Please take away any painful memories as well as my desire to be with my loved one."

3. Forgive Everyone.

If your loved one's death is not a natural death, try to forgive everyone who is responsible for the death of your loved one. If it was caused by an accident or other tragic events, ask the Lord what you can do to forgive and reconcile with others. Have compassion for yourself and others who may be related to the death of your loved one.

(1) Have peace: Having peace does not mean that you have to reconcile with everyone face to face. It means you have accepted the reality of the loss, but you do not hold any resentment or anger toward anyone. Prayer: "Holy Spirit, guide and direct me with your wisdom and strength. Help me to do what I need to do to find peace and healing, so I can come out of this fire with strength and courage. Lord Jesus, please heal my memories of the painful death of my loved one. Help me to forgive everyone who is related to my loved one's death. I let go of my resentment, bitterness, and anger."

(2) Forgive everyone including yourself: You need to let go of all resentment, anger, and bitterness toward anyone associated with your loved one's death. One by one, tell God that you forgive your loved one or others who are involved. Prayer: "God, I release all my anger, resentment, bitterness, and my unforgiving spirit. Take away all of my thoughts that are hindering the healing process of my soul and spirit. Please forgive me, if I have sinned against you and others. I forgive everyone who is responsible for my loved one's death. Bless them and forgive them." *(Matthew 5:4, 1 John 4:20)*

(3) Let go of your expectations: Don't expect others to understand your pain and meet your needs. Many people don't know how to help those who are grieving. By letting go of your expectations of how others should help you, you will be freed from a unforgiving, and critical spirits.

(4) <u>Start your relationship with Jesus</u>: If you do not have a relationship with Jesus, this is an opportunity to invite Him into your heart. Prayer: "Lord Jesus, I invite you into my heart and my life. I give my heart to you. Forgive all my sins. Lord, I am hurting, but I believe that you can heal my broken heart. Fill my heart with your joy and peace. If there is any area that I need to work on, please show me. I pray this in Jesus' name. Amen."

<u>4. Keep working on healing of your heart</u>.

(1) <u>Do something to forget about your loss</u>: Take a break to enjoy the small things in life: enjoying nature, driving in the countryside, drawing, exercise, dancing, taking a trip, or enjoying godly humor. Avoid alcohol, drugs, violence, or following destructive paths to avoid the pain. Or you will create more tornadoes, it will delay healing and the end result can be devastating.

(2) <u>Find supportive friends</u>: Find people who will listen and understand your situation, struggles, and feelings. Attend church to get to know God and to experience love, support, and healing. Find friends with healing lessons to share.

(3) <u>Join a grief support group or start one if you can't find one</u>: Find people who have walked this similar path and have learned the lessons and can guide you to experience healing from grief. Pray for each other's healing. *"Is any one of you in trouble? He should pray. Is anyone happy? Let him sing songs of praise. Is any one of you sick? He should call the elders of the church to pray over him and anoint him with oil in the name of the Lord. And the prayer offered in faith will make the sick person well; the Lord will raise him up. If he has sinned, he will be forgiven. Therefore confess your sins to each other and pray for each other so that you may be healed. The prayer of a righteous man is powerful and effective."* (James 5:13-16)

(4) <u>Help others who are hurting</u>: As you help others, your pain

will start to look small. You will see that you are not alone. There are many who carry more pain than you do. Paul teaches us to help each other. *"Carry each other's burdens, and in this way you will fulfill the law of Christ."* (Galatians 6:2) Write a testimony or book about how God has helped you in your grieving process so you can encourage others. Your story of tears will bring healing to others, and, *"Those who sow in tears will reap with songs of joy. He who goes out weeping, carrying seed to sow, will return with songs of joy, carrying sheaves with him."* (Psalm 126:5-6) You will know that God comforts those who are hurting. *"Praise be to the God and Father of our Lord Jesus Christ, the Father of compassion and the God of all comfort, who comforts us in all our troubles, so that we can comfort those in any trouble with the comfort we ourselves have received from God."* (2 Corinthians 1:3-4)

5. What happens when you are healed?

When you are healed, you are not immersed in grief and pain from your loss. Your heart is filled with gratitude, thankfulness toward God. You will have compassion toward others who are hurting. You will be free from the triggers of grief and pain, and be able to function normally. You will be amazed at how much God can bring healing to your broken heart. You will learn to be content with what you have. You will filled with joy and peace.

"The Lord will surely comfort Zion and will look with compassion on all her ruins; he will make her deserts like Eden, her wastelands like the garden of the Lord. Joy and gladness will be found in her, thanksgiving and the sound of singing." (Isaiah 51:3)

Note: To learn how to process grief and loss, read the book, *Dancing in the Sky, A Story of Hope for Grieving Hearts.*

Chapter 15

How to Process Trauma

1. Have faith in God.

As you have read in the many stories in this book, tornadoes of life tragedies can be very damaging to souls like poison. But we can trust God in any situation because He has the power to heal us. Our Lord Jesus deeply cares for us and He has all the power to heal us.

Healing may take time because healing is a process but God can heal a wounded person. God can revive a person who feels like dying because of their traumatic experiences. In order to be healed, we need to exercise our faith. We also need to process hurting and pain and letting go of them.

2. Find answers from the Word of God.

The lessons we can learn in life's crises are found in the Scriptures and God's Word has all the answers for healing of our souls. God's Word is medicine for poisoned souls. Our healing of mind and heart depends on how we walk with Jesus everyday as we pray and rely on His Word. How can we have a close relationship with Jesus? I ask you to read the Gospels (Matthew, Mark, Luke, John) for 30 minutes and pray 30 minutes (talk to God 15 minutes and practice silence 15 minutes) every day for the next 30 days so you can get to know Jesus and develop a habit of reading and praying to experience healing from hurt, pain and trauma.

People who are traumatized are vulnerable to spiritual attack and they need to learn how to guard themselves. Paul gives us clear instructions on how to be strong in the Lord.

Prayer: "Lord Jesus, please give me the discernment to understand the Bible so I can get to know you and your love and power to heal my mind and soul."

3. Practice silence.

Jesus calmed the sea by saying, "Be still." We need to say to ourselves, "Be still." to calm our minds as much as we can especially in times of turmoil and pain. The Scripture says, *"Be still before the LORD and wait patiently for him." (Psalm 37:7a)*

Silence brings healing when we are hurting. Many traumatized people suffer from bad voices which are negative and destructive voices. You can control your mind by learning to silence your thoughts.

4. Pray for healing.

Spend time in prayer whenever you can. You can pray throughout the day and focus on what God can do for you.

Prayer: "Lord Jesus, all things are possible through you. Please heal my heart with the power of the Holy Spirit. Help me to forgive everyone who hurt me. I give you all my painful memories and thoughts. Please help me to be free from any negative voices. I will not grieve with sad feelings or ponder my past any more. Help me to look up to you every moment. I ask you to give me a new heart and make me into the person that you want me to be. I ask you for forgiveness for holding any resentment, hate or anger. I give up all my bad attitudes toward all who have hurt me. I forgive everyone including myself. Please heal my memory so I don't suffer from triggers and flashbacks any more. Fill my heart with your peace and joy. Please heal me so I can help others. Amen."

5. Meditate on the Scriptures.

Find the Bible verses that touch you and meditate on them everyday. The following Scriptures have helped me in my troubled times.

Jesus said, *"Do not let your hearts be troubled. Trust in God; trust also in me. In my Father's house are many rooms; if it were not so, I would have told you. I am going there to prepare a place for you. And if I go and prepare a place for you, I will come back and take you to be with me that you also may be where I* am." (John 14:1-3)

"When you pass through the waters, I will be with you; and when you pass through the rivers, they will not sweep over you. When you walk through the fire, you will not be burned; the flames will not set you ablaze." (Isaiah 43:2)

"Do you not know? Have you not heard? The Lord is the everlasting God, the Creator of the ends of the earth. He will not grow tired or weary, and his understanding no one can fathom. He gives strength to the weary and increases the power of the weak. Even youths grow tired and weary, and young men stumble and fall; but those who hope in the Lord will renew their strength. They will soar on wings like eagles; they will run and not grow weary, they will walk and not be faint." (Isaiah 40:28-31)

"So do not fear, for I am with you; do not be dismayed, for I am your God. I will strengthen you and help you; I will uphold you with my righteous right hand." (Isaiah 41:10)

"Jesus replied, 'What is impossible with men is possible with God.'" (Luke 18:27)

"If that is how God clothes the grass of the field, which is here today and tomorrow is thrown into the fire, will he not much more clothe you, O you of little faith? So do not worry, saying, 'What shall we eat?' or 'What shall we drink?' or 'What shall we wear?' For the pagans run after all these things, and your heavenly Father knows that you need them. But seek first his kingdom and his righteousness, and all these things will be given to you as well. Therefore do not worry about tomorrow, for tomorrow will worry about itself. Each day has enough trouble of its own." (Matthew 6:30-34)

"Be strong and courageous, because you will lead these people to inherit the land I swore to their forefathers to give them. Be strong and very courageous. Be careful to obey all the law my servant Moses gave you; do not turn from it to the right or to the left, that you may be successful wherever you go. Do not let this Book of the Law depart from your mouth; meditate on it day and night, so that you may be careful to do everything written in it. Then you will be prosperous and successful. Have I not commanded you? Be strong and courageous. Do not be terrified; do not be discouraged, for the LORD your God will be with you wherever you go." (Joshua 1:6-9)

"What, then, shall we say in response to this?
If God is for us, who can be against us?
He who did not spare his own Son,
but gave him up for us all —
how will he not also, along with him,
graciously give us all things?
Who will bring any charge against
those whom God has chosen?
It is God who justifies.
Who is he that condemns?
Christ Jesus, who died —
more than that, who was raised to life —
is at the right hand of God
and is also interceding for us.
Who shall separate us from the love of Christ?
Shall trouble or hardship or persecution
or famine or nakedness or danger or sword?
As it is written:
'For your sake we face death all day long;
we are considered as sheep to be slaughtered.'
No, in all these things we are more than
conquerors through him who loved us.
For I am convinced that neither death nor life,
neither angels nor demons, neither the present
nor the future, nor any powers, neither height
nor depth, nor anything else in all creation,
will be able to separate us from the love of God
that is in Christ Jesus our Lord."
(Romans 8:31-39)

6. Avoid alcohol or drugs or any addiction to numb your pain.

This will only delay your healing. Try to find positive groups like church and attend worship services and Bible studies to find healing through God and others who have experienced healing. Try to surround yourself with positive people and avoid any negative people so you can experience healing instead of hurting.

7. Find pastors or counselors for continued healing.

There are others who are trained to help you in your healing process like pastors, chaplains, and other mature Christians. Contact them and ask them to pray for you. Contact professional counselors if you need help.

8. Surround yourself with positive people.

Some people will drag you down, and hurt you more than help you. They create tornadoes in our lives. Ask the Lord for discernment so you are not in a place where you can be hurt by others. Find people who are loving and caring. Stay away from any people with low moral values who don't have any respect for themselves or others. This will prevent you from some tornados caused by other situations. There are some tornadoes beyond your control, but try to prevent the ones you can control. Attend church and find people who have high moral values. Not all the people who attend church have high moral values either so be careful with whom you associate. Sometimes it will be best to find places where people are helping others. So, volunteer for church and community organizations where there are people who have the goal of helping others who are hurting. The more you focus on helping others instead of trying to get others to meet your needs, the more you will experience healing.

Prayer: "Lord Jesus, help me to have the wisdom to stay away from places and people who will cause tornadoes in my life. Help me to live a peaceful life by surrounding myself with people who create peace not tornadoes. Amen."

9. Write a journal.

Write a journal and your story about how God has helped you. This will help you process your deep wounds and will bring healing in your mind.

10. Find music for healing of mind.

Find some inspirational music which can help you focus

on God and healing. Inspirational music brings healing.

11. Proclaim victory.

In everything, proclaim victory in Christ. Write a victory prayer for yourself. Jesus said, "*I have told you these things, so that in me you may have peace. In this world you will have trouble. But take heart! I have overcome the world.*" (John 16:33)

John wrote, "*You, dear children, are from God and have overcome them, because the one who is in you is greater than the one who is in the world.*" (1 John 4:4) "*For everyone born of God overcomes the world. This is the victory that has overcome the world, even our faith. Who is it that overcomes the world? Only he who believes that Jesus is the Son of God.*" (1 John 5:4-5)

12. Share your story with others.

God can use your painful tornado story to help others who are in a similar situation. Many are in need of guidance and healing. Start sharing your tornado story and the lessons you have learned and how you were able to move on. This will give others hope that they too can experience healing and can move on.

Chapter 16

Spiritual Healing:
Nightmares, Hurtful Voices and Confusion

Anyone can have spiritual encounters because we are living in both a physical and a spiritual world. No one is exempt from stepping into the realm of the spiritual world. We can learn to find peace and healing from it with God's help. However, there are people who experience the spiritual world more than others and they are troubled by it. I have learned that the following group of people have a greater tendency to be bothered by spirits or spiritual world bringing confusion, fear, and nightmares:

(1) Those traumatized by abuse or have seen others being abused.
(2) Those who suffered from terrorizing events such as war or have seen the traumatic deaths of others.
(3) Those who have experienced traumatic or devastating death or loss such as suicide or brutality.
(4) Those who are involved in Satanic ritual or cult.
(5) People who use alcohol, drugs, or other addictive substances which can affect their mind.

1. Nightmares

Some people, awake or asleep can hear, see and feel bad spirits not only in their minds, but also with their physical senses. This sounds scary but it happens to some people.

I believe nightmarish dreams are not natural but it is caused by tormenting spirits. These spirits attack people and try to choke them not only in their sleep but while they are awake. With God's help, you can be freed from these bad spirits and nightmares. If you have problems like that, you don't have to be scared.

In my earlier years, I have seen scary looking spirits working in people and the spirits attacked me physically to the point of exhaustion. I also suffered from terrible nightmares after my sister died in a car accident. I was afraid to go to sleep because I felt spirits choking me and I had a difficult time breathing in my dream and had a difficult time waking up.

I didn't know what was happening. My mother told me that it was a spiritual attack and I need to pray more so I don't have nightmares any more. She was right. As I started reading the Bible and prayed more and relied on God for spiritual healing, He delivered me from nightmares and spiritual attacks. I am not afraid of these attacks anymore because I learned how the demons try to scare me. I can win and overcome them with God's help.

If you are suffering from nightmares, start reading the Bible and praying "The Lord's Prayer." Keep praying until you can find peace. Many nightmares are spiritual encounters with bad spirits.

Prayer: "Lord Jesus, I believe that you have the power to help me and release me from nightmares. I ask you to help me to be strong so I can win this spiritual battle with your power. Please surround me with angels and protect me day and night from bad spirits. I ask for forgiveness if I have sinned against you and others. If there is any sin I need to repent, please help me to repent. Thank you for your forgiveness. I forgive everyone who has sinned against me. Help me to love you and serve you as you want me to. I pray for the salvation of all my family and relatives and others who don't know you. I pray this in Jesus' name. Amen."

Note: If you suffer from nightmares, read the book, *Dreams and Interpretation, Healing from Nightmares* to learn how to overcome nightmares.

2. The hurtful voices

Many people suffer from hearing negative and destructive voices and thoughts that come to their mind and some even hear it audibly. How do you deal with these destructive, negative, hurtful voices?

First, you need to realize from where these voices come. When people hear voices in their mind, many think these are their own voices or thoughts. That's not always true. There are four voices people hear in their minds: 1) Their own voice; 2) The voices of other people; 3) A bad voice (The devil's destructive voice; 4) A good voice (God's voice).

Other people's voices may be something that we remember from the past and it could be good or bad. Our own voice is our own thoughts, which can be good or bad. We have freedom to make choices about which voices we will accept and this will determine how we think and how we live. If we accept bad voices, we will be in turmoil and could fall into sin by following them. If we accept good voices which is God's voice, we will find comfort and healing.

Where do you think the devil attacks first? It's our mind where we hear bad, wrong, negative, destructive, and sinful voices. They need to be resisted by rebuking them in the name of Jesus, and replacing them with the life-giving, positive Word of God.

People who have suffered from depression and suicidal thoughts have shared with me that they have heard many bad voices telling them how bad and worthless they are and sometimes give directions on how to hurt themselves and others.

Peter warns us about the spiritual attack. He wrote, *"Be self-controlled and alert. Your enemy the devil prowls around like a roaring lion looking for someone to devour. Resist him, standing firm in the faith, because you know that your brothers throughout the world are undergoing the same kind of sufferings. And the God of all grace, who called you to his eternal glory in Christ, after you have suffered a little while, will himself restore you and make you strong, firm and steadfast. To him be the power for ever and ever. Amen." (1 Peter 5:8-11)*

Prayer: "Lord Jesus, please help me to have discernment; to know what is a good voice or a bad voice, so I can follow the Holy Spirit's voice. I ask for your guidance and wisdom to follow you and learn to resist destructive voices."

If you have been involved in Satanic cult rituals and have turned to God, but you suffer from a destructive voice say that God cannot forgive you, know that God has forgiven you. Don't believe any voices undermining God's love for you. I encourage you to memorize the following Scripture: and recite it whenever you feel you need God's comfort: *"The Spirit of the Lord is on me, because he has anointed me to preach good news to the poor. He has sent me to proclaim freedom for the prisoners and recovery of sight for the blind, to release the oppressed, to proclaim the year of the Lord's favor." (Luke 4:18-19)*

Here is a prayer for those who want to turn to God for healing. Prayer: "Jesus, I invite you to be the Lord and Savior of my life. I ask for your forgiveness for seeking other spirits which are hurting me and tormenting me. Please forgive all my sins and cleanse me. I believe in the power of your blood which was shed on the cross for my sins. Bless me with the Holy Spirit and clothe me with the armor of God. Surround me with angels to protect me from the devil's lies and attack. I believe you died on the cross and shed your blood to forgive me. Thank you for your forgiveness. Help me so I can win this spiritual battle with your power. Bless me with wisdom and discernment so I can understand the Bible. I pray this in Jesus' name. Amen."

Note: To learn how to control of your thoughts and be freed from tormenting voices, read the book, *Four Voices, How They Affect Our Mind; How to Overcome Self-destructive Voices and Hear the Nurturing Voice of God.*

3. Spiritual confusion

Not all spiritual encounters are bad; some are from the

Lord. God can give us spiritual visions about our loved ones who passed away, to give us comfort and healing. What God gives us is always good and helps us to grow in faith. He would not scare us by showing dead people walking in daylight or through nightmares.

However, there are some people who see dead people in physical forms and this encounter brings turmoil to the point that they may wonder if they are going crazy. They are not crazy. They are seeing the spiritual world which is hidden to many, but they are seeing, feeling and hearing it. This spiritual encounter is caused by demons who are trying to confuse people. Bad spirits can disguise themselves as the deceased person and appear to some people.

When people die, their spirits are no longer here. Jesus tells a story of where dead peoples' spirits are. *Luke 16:19-31* tells us the story of Lazarus and the rich man. The rich man who was tormented in hell, asked Abraham to send Lazarus to warn people so they don't have to be in the place of torment, but his request was not granted.

Avoid talking to a dead person's spirit because the Lord tells us not to communicate with them. *"Do not turn to mediums or seek out spiritists, for you will be defiled by them. I am the Lord your God."* *(Leviticus 19:31)*

Mediums in this context are people who seek to talk to the spirits of dead people. Demons can disguise themselves to look like a dead person to deceive us. If that happens and you are scared, then rebuke that spirit. James wrote, *"Submit yourselves, then, to God. Resist the devil, and he will flee from you."* *(James 4:7)* So, resist them by saying, "In the name of Jesus, leave from me. I am a child of God."

Prayer: "Lord Jesus, I believe in you. I ask you to surround me with angels and protect me from confusing spirits. Help me to love you and serve you. Bless me with peace that you only can give. I pray this in Jesus' name. Amen."

Chapter 17

A Victory Prayer

I wrote a prayer of victory to be healed from anxiety attacks. Whenever the spirits of fear and anxiety try to take over my mind, I claim victory in Christ. This prayer has helped me immensely and I have not had an anxiety attack since I started proclaiming victory in Christ. Write your own prayer of victory and start proclaiming victory in your life. Here is the victory prayer I wrote:

1. A victory prayer for myself
I claim victory that I made a decision to love Jesus.
He is the first priority in my life.
I claim victory for God because He has the ultimate power over everything in my life, no one else does.
I claim victory because I made a commitment to serve Christ.
I claim victory over my guilt and shame because all my sins are washed away by the blood of Jesus Christ
I claim victory that God is the source of my love, peace, wisdom, joy, and strength.
I claim victory over my future belief that
God is going to bless me beyond my imagination.
I claim victory because I decided to love Jesus more than my sinful desires and passion.
I claim victory over all my problems and concerns
so that I am continuously surrendering everything to God.
I claim victory that I made a decision to bless and forgive those who have hurt me.
I claim victory over my fears because God is guiding
my spiritual path.
I claim victory over my life challenges knowing that
God is going to give me wisdom to handle them.

2. A victory prayer for my family

I claim victory that God will take care of my family
for His glory.
I claim victory that my family will be filled with
the Holy Spirit and serve God to the fullest.
I claim victory that God will give my children spiritual
blessings beyond my imagination.
I claim victory for my children that God will provide what they
need, including godly mentors.
I claim victory that my family will be blessed with
spiritual gifts and use them for God's glory.
I claim victory that God will take care of my family
when I cannot take care of them.
I claim victory that God will protect my family and
help them grow in faith.
I claim victory that other people will be blessed by
my family's presence and ministry.

3. A victory prayer for my ministry

I claim victory that God will provide an opportunity
for me to spread the gospel of Jesus much more than
I have ever imagined.
I claim victory that with God's help, I will be able to help others
use their spiritual gifts to the maximum for God's glory.
I claim victory that the Holy Spirit will bring powerful Christian
leaders to join me in building up the kingdom
of God to win many lost souls and help them grow spiritually.
I claim victory that God will help me use my time wisely
to reach out to those who are in spiritual bondage,
so they can find spiritual freedom in Christ.
I claim victory because I am continuously surrendering
all my plans and desires in order to love and serve Christ.
I claim victory in managing financial resources with God's
wisdom so that I will glorify God with my resources and help
others to be saved and find hope and healing in Christ.
I claim victory that the Holy Spirit will anoint me so much that

others will experience the Holy Spirit's healing presence through my ministry and book projects.

I claim victory that when God has different ministry plans for my life, I will obey Him because His plans are always better than mine.

I claim victory over my selfishness that I will look after Jesus' interest, knowing that is the only way to build up Christ's kingdom.

I claim victory because I will be focusing all my gifts, time, energy on loving Jesus and serving Him to the fullest.

Chapter 18

An Invitation

1. An Invitation to Accept Christ

Do you have an empty heart that cannot be filled with anyone or anything? God can fill your empty heart with His love and forgiveness. Do you feel your life has no meaning, no direction, no purpose, and you don't know where to turn to find the answers? It's time to turn to God. That's the only way you will understand the meaning and the purpose of your life. You will find direction that will lead you to fulfillment and joy. Is your heart broken and hurting, and you don't know how to experience healing? Until we meet Christ in our hearts, we cannot find the peace and healing that God can provide. Jesus can help heal your broken heart. If you don't have a relationship with Christ, this is an opportunity for you to accept Jesus into your heart so you can be saved, find peace and healing from God. Here is a prayer if you are ready to accept Jesus:

Prayer: "Dear Jesus, I surrender my life and everything to you. I give you all my pain, fear, regret, resentment, anger, worry, and concerns that overwhelm me. I am a sinner. I need your forgiveness. Please come into my heart and my life and forgive all my sins. I believe that you died for my sins and that you have plans for my life. Please heal my broken heart and bless me with your peace and joy. Help me to cleanse my life so I can live a godly life. Help me to understand your plans for my life and help me to obey you. Fill me with the Holy Spirit, and guide me so I can follow your way. I pray this in Jesus' name. Amen."

2. An Invitation for The Transformation Project Prison Ministry (TPPM).

Books and DVDs produced by TPPM are distributed in many jails, prisons, and homeless shelters nationwide free of charge made possible by grants and donations. America has 2.3 million people incarcerated, the largest prison population in the world, and there is a great shortage of inspirational books in many jails and prisons.

"One Million Dream Project"

In 2010, TPPM board decided to expand the ministry goal, and started the "One Million Dream Project." TPPM decided to raise enough funds to distribute one million copies of each book that TPPM has produced for prisoners and homeless people. I ask you to pray for this project so God can help TPPM to reach out to those who cannot speak for themselves, and are in need of spiritual guidance.

TPPM is a 501(c)(3) nonprofit organization, so your donation is 100% tax deductible. If you would like to be a partner in this very important mission of bringing transformation through the message of Christ in prisons and homeless shelters, or want to know more about this project, please visit: www.maximumsaints.org.

You can donate on line or write a check addressed to:

Transformation Project Prison Ministry
5209 Montview Boulevard
Denver, CO 80207

Website: www.maximumsaints.org
Facebook: http://tinyurl.com/yhhcp5g
Email: maximumsaints@maximumsaints.org

3. How to purchase *Maximum Saints* Books

This is for individuals who would like to purchase or send a copy to their incarcerated family. TPPM receives lots of requests for individual distribution but we only distribute them through chaplains. All the proceeds from *Maximum Saints* will go to TPPM to distribute more free books and DVDs to prisons and homeless shelters.

To find out more about purchasing *Maximum Saints* books, check our website: www.maximumsaints.org. The following books are available:

Book One: *Maximum Saints Never Hide in the Dark*
Book Two: *Maximum Saints Make No Little Plans*
Book Three: *Maximum Saints Dream*
Book Four: *Maximum Saints Forgive*
Book Five: *Maximum Saints All Things Are Possible*

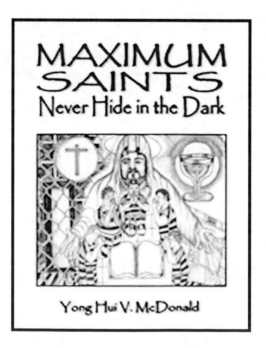

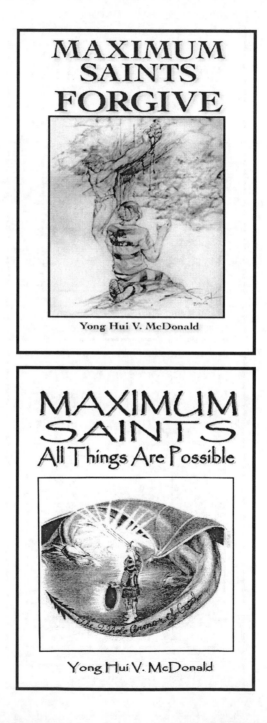

ABOUT THE AUTHOR

Yong Hui V. McDonald, also known as Vescinda McDonald, is a chaplain at Adams County Detention Facility, certified American Correctional Chaplain, spiritual director and on-call hospital chaplain. She founded the Transformation Project Prison Ministry (TPPM) in 2005 and founded GriefPathway Ventures, LLC in 2010 to help others learn how to process grief and healing. In 2011, she founded Veterans Twofish Foundation, a 501(c)(3) nonprofit, to provide inspirational resources to veterans.

Education:
- Multnomah Bible College, B.A.B.E. (1984)
- Iliff School of Theology, Master of Divinity (2002)

Books and Audio Books Written by Yong Hui V. McDonald:
- *Moment by Moment*
- *Journey With Jesus, Visions, Dreams, Meditations & Reflections*
- *Dancing in the Sky, A Story of Hope for Grieving Hearts*
- *Twisted Logic, The Shadow of Suicide*
- *Twisted Logic, The Window of Depression*
- *Dreams & Interpretations, Healing from Nightmares*
- *I Was The Mountain, In Search of Faith & Revival*
- *The Ultimate Parenting Guide, How to Enjoy Peaceful Parenting and Joyful Children*
- *Prisoners Victory Parade, Extraordinary Stories of Maximum Saints & Former Prisoners*
- *Four Voices, How They Affect Our Minds: How to Overcome Self-Destructive Voices and Hear the Nurturing Voice of God*
- *Tornadoes, Grief, Loss, Trauma, and PTSD: Tornadoes, Lessons, Teaching – The TLT Model for Healing*
- Compiled and published five *Maximum Saints* books under the Transformation Project Prison Ministry.

DVDs produced by Yong Hui:
- *Dancing in The Sky, Mismatched Shoes*

- *Tears of The Dragonfly, Suicide and Suicide Prevention (CD* is also available)

Spanish books produced by Yong Hui:
- *Twisted Logic, The Shadow of Suicide*
- *Journey With Jesus, Visions, Dreams, Meditations & Reflections*

GriefPathway Ventures, LLC,
P.O. Box 220
Brighton, CO 80601
Website: www.griefpathway.com
Email: griefpwv@gmail.com

Veterans Twofish Foundation
P.O. Box 220
Brighton, CO 80601
Website: www.veteranstwofish.org
Email: griefpwv@gmail.com

CPSIA information can be obtained at www.ICGtesting.com
Printed in the USA
LVOW101326140812

294290LV00005B/20/P